"Few other large cities on planet Earth are experi[...]
their diverse Christian leadership communities [...]
in New York City. Read this and judge for you[...]
    Bill Hybels, founder and senior pastor,
    chairman of t[...]

"Global cities present simultaneously some of the greatest challenges and opportunities for the gospel. The Lausanne Movement is thankful for Mac's influential voice as a Lausanne catalyst for global cities and for the many remarkable stories and statistics shared in this book. . . . I encourage all leaders who care about the advance of the gospel to read this."
    Michael Oh, executive director/CEO, Lausanne Movement

"If you're wondering whether the Christian movement is over, read *A Disruptive Gospel*. What Luke did for the first century, Dr. Mac Pier has done for the twenty-first century. I consider Mac the greatest authority on global Christian expansion today and was deeply moved by his firsthand account of God's astonishing work in global cities. As an eyewitness to this miraculous movement in Dallas and New York City, I can tell you that Mac's portraits are not only accurate but also transforming. Read *A Disruptive Gospel* and join the awakening of our age."
    James C. Denison, PhD, CEO and cofounder, Denison Forum
    on Truth and Culture

"Mac tells the brilliant story of how the love of Christ "disrupts" neighborhoods, cities, and nations when God's people join together and ask, "What does my city need, and how can I serve?" He bears witness to beautiful gospel movement stories from cities all over the world that are equal parts passion and practicality."
    Kevin Palau, CEO, Luis Palau Association; author of *Unlikely*

"I have known Mac Pier for years and can't think of anyone more qualified to mobilize and equip Christian leaders with the tools to transform our cities. I highly recommend this important book to anyone who wants to be a part of creating social change. Get ready to be disrupted!"
    Brenda Salter McNeil, author, *Roadmap to Reconciliation*

"After more than fifty years of struggling to find the right solution to rescue our cities, Mac Pier has given us the solution. We must become disruptive agents of God to erase the status quo and create cities that represent God's universal agenda."
    Dr. W. Wilson Goode Sr., director and organizer, Amachi, Inc.; former mayor,
    city of Philadelphia

"If the native New Yorkers give the city its solidity, the commuters give the city its velocity, and the immigrants give the city its dreams, then this book gives us a resource that will help accelerate the mission to reach the world through its cities."
    Ram Gidoomal, Commander of the Most Excellent Order of the British
    Empire; chairman, the Lausanne Movement International Board

"Mac Pier and I have journeyed together for more than twenty years. This story tells the profound and remarkable ways God has disrupted New York City. I've seen it. Read and be inspired for your city."
    Steve Bell, executive vice president, Willow Creek Association

"Mac Pier is one of the pioneers of the movement of the gospel happening in New York today. And he has taken what he has learned and has cultivated a passion for gospel movements in cities around the world. More than just a book of theory, this is a real-life handbook of what God is doing in the world today. A vital and important read."

Jon Tyson, founding pastor, Trinity Grace Church New York

"When Jason is dragged before the rulers of the city in first-century Thessalonica, he is accused of assisting those who brought the transforming power of the gospel to that city. The charge is telling: "These who have turned the world upside down have come here too" (Acts 17:6 NKJV). I believe the gospel has the ability to disrupt every facet of city life as it turns this world right side up! By creating a city-gospel-context and tangible, real-world examples of its impact, I believe this book is a catalyst for disrupting apathy and passivity, thus catapulting the church into the incredible opportunity global urbanization provides!"

Jurie Kriel, Doxa Deo and the City Changers Movement

"The gospel of Christ is alive and well, but make no mistake, it is disruptive. Mac Pier communicates with power and clarity the essence of what God is doing around the globe in the most impactful and vulnerable cities in the world. An unbridled movement is gaining momentum, and the message of Jesus is the power of this transformation—not in spite of the chaos in the world, but in the middle of it. God is igniting His work. He is disrupting the status quo. He's redeeming and rescuing. *A Disruptive Gospel* reads like the book of Acts, but then again, the gospel is still the bedrock for rebuilding any and every city on the planet. Prepare to be inspired."

Dan Wolgemuth, president/CEO, Youth for Christ USA

"In *A Disruptive Gospel*, Mac gives us a front-row seat, refreshes our imagination, and ignites a passion to the vision cast by Stott and Graham to take the whole gospel to the whole world by the whole church."

Daryl Heald, founder, Generous Giving

"*A Disruptive Gospel* possesses the stories to infuse you with passion and the prophetic strategies to see gospel movements flourish in cities around the globe. It's a must-read for all those who are serious about what God is doing now and who desire a peek into what God is about to do in cities across the earth."

Rev. Adam Durso, DD, CEO, Catalytic Consulting NYC.

"The implementation of the principles in *A Disruptive Gospel* will culminate into a movement that is progressive but not without difficulty. It will be unstoppable, unmovable, and unshakable—the veritable kingdom of God on earth as it is always in heaven."

Sheila Bailey, founder and president, Sheila B. Ministries

"Passion. Vision. Purpose. Challenge. In *A Disruptive Gospel*, each of these words leaps off the page with accounts of what God is doing in cities around the world. This book is a call to action. . . . This book will sow ideas and strategies for everyone who reads it."

Jerry E. White, PhD, international president emeritus, The Navigators; major general, USAF; retired chairman, Lausanne Workplace Network

A DISRUPTIVE GOSPEL

STORIES AND STRATEGIES
FOR TRANSFORMING YOUR CITY

MAC PIER

BakerBooks

a division of Baker Publishing Group
Grand Rapids, Michigan

Published by Baker Books
a division of Baker Publishing Group
P.O. Box 6287, Grand Rapids, MI 49516-6287
www.bakerbooks.com

Printed in the United States of America

The Library of Congress Cataloging-in-Publication Data is on file at the Library of Congress, Washington, DC.

ISBN 978-0-8010-1920-3 | ISBN 978-0-8010-7520-9 (cloth)

16 17 18 19 20 21 22   7 6 5 4 3 2 1

In Dedication

To a very special group of friends who have demonstrated
that the gospel grows at the speed of friendship

Raymond and Marydel
Bob and Leslie
D. G. and Gini
Ray and Denise
Mario and Lynelle
Katherine and Alan
Zach and Regan
Scott and Holly
Craig and Laura
Dave and Carol
David
Paul

CONTENTS

Contents

FOREWORD

THE GOSPEL IS DISRUPTING CITIES

The book you are about to read is one more volume about the gospel. You may say, "I know the gospel," but since the gospel is endlessly rich and infinitely multifaceted, there is always something new to learn about its power and effect (1 Pet. 1:12).

In these pages Mac shows how the gospel has the power to disrupt the status quo, which is always indifferent to evil. The gospel disrupted the life of a complacent teenager in South Dakota. It disrupted a cold, hard resistance to the historic gospel in the boroughs of New York City and the center of Manhattan. It disrupted the high walls between denominations and the even higher walls between the races and classes to form an unprecedented unity and movement to reach the metro region of New York. And it has begun to make use of the new and close connections between the great global cities of the world to spread many of these same influences and effects to other urban centers. This is the story of all that, and—if you are a Christian minister or lay leader—you could hardly find a more encouraging book to read today.

I can imagine skepticism regarding the claims about what God is doing and will do in cities. Don't all the headlines tell us that Christianity, and even belief in God in general, is in retreat, especially among the young millennial generation and in the centers of Western secular culture—the great cities? Aren't the cities of Europe, for example, filled with empty church buildings that are being turned into nightclubs, restaurants, and condos? Isn't religion in a downward arc of inevitable decline?

No. Last year those of us who were at a European church planters' conference in Paris were addressed by Grace Davie, emeritus professor of sociology at the University of Exeter in Great Britain. She pointed out that, yes, nominal or inherited Christianity is declining. By this she meant religion people are born into, so that one might say, for example, "I'm Norwegian, so I'm Lutheran" or "I'm French, so I'm Catholic." We live in modern societies where we are taught the importance of our own free choices. Inherited religion no longer maintains its hold on most people. This is why, overall, fewer people who are born into a church-connected family end up attending and belonging to those congregations.

However, she noted (against all expectations) that new movements of Christian faith are growing in Western cities. One reason for this is the influx of Christians from the global south. In China, Africa, and many other places in the world, Christianity is growing rapidly as those societies are modernizing. Then, as people come to Europe and the United States from Africa, Latin America, and Asia, they plant new churches or strengthen other ones that are growing and reaching those cities. Why? Because, while religion that is inherited will decline in the modern age, religion that is *chosen* will not. The growing Christian churches are evangelical and Pentecostal, and they emphasize the biblical call to "choose for yourselves this day whom you will serve" (Josh. 24:15) and the biblical teaching that we stand or fall on our own faith, not the choices of our family or community (Ezek. 18). These churches teach that vicarious, formal religion is not enough. There must be a radical, inward conversion (Deut. 30:6; Jer. 9:25; Rom. 2:29). Christianity that foregrounds these important biblical concepts and lifts up heart-changing personal faith can reach many contemporary people—and it can reach cities.

Davie, a sociologist, observed that much of the new Christian movement and growth is coming into various nations through their greatest cities. New spiritual vitality is coming to Europe and parts of the United States that way, and Christianity is also coming to non-Christian countries through their chief urban areas. While cities, she says, have in the past been seen as the "beacons of a more irreligious future," now it is in the cities that Christianity is thriving because they are more multiethnic and more globalized, and the new kinds of faith that call modern people to decide and choose are being deployed there. Davie added, as an example, that London now has more growing churches than anywhere else in Great Britain.

This message is both exciting and challenging for Christians in cities today. In Western countries, many of the older churches relying on inherited faith are dying. Gone is that great "canopy" of nominal Christians who were not personally devout but thought religion was good and important and were not very difficult to draw into Christian churches. However, contemporary people have plenty of the same intuitions of God and sin and spiritual longings for love, meaning, and grace that their ancestors did. Some people will hear the same message and say, "You are out of your mind!" (Acts 26:24), while others will be cut to the heart and ask, "What shall we do?" (2:37).

How can believers and church leaders in the cities of the world meet this challenge and seize this opportunity? They can start by grasping and building on the five truths and priorities Mac explains and illustrates throughout this book:

The Gospel Matters. There is the power. Know, believe, and lift up the gospel, and everything will change.

Church Unity Matters. Denominations and traditions complement and supplement one another. No one church or kind of church alone can reach the city.

Cities Matter. The people of the world are moving into cities faster than the church is. No mission is more imperative than multiplying churches and ministry in urban areas.

Millennial Leadership Matters. These great challenges will not be met unless the reins of leadership are passed to this generation now.

Finally, *Movement Matters*. What is a movement? It's actually not easy to define. But if by faithful ministry you release the power of the gospel and bring the churches and generations together in prayer and ingenuity to reach your city—well, you'll know a movement when you see it.

Tim Keller, January 2016

ACKNOWLEDGMENTS

I want to thank several people who helped make this book possible.

Thanks to the team at Baker Publishing, especially Brian Smith and Brian Thomasson.

Thanks to Tina Jacobson and Dan Balow for their encouragement and advocacy.

Thanks to my wife, Marya, who loves me so well and loves our shared calling.

Thanks to the New York City Leadership Center board and staff, who labor so hard on behalf of a shared vision to catalyze leaders to impact their cities.

Thanks to the many friends who allowed me to hear their stories. My prayer is that this book tells those stories well.

Thanks most of all to God, who has disrupted the world with the gospel in the person of Jesus.

1

A DISRUPTED LIFE

SEEDS OF A MOVEMENT

As he neared Damascus on his journey, suddenly a light from heaven flashed around him. He fell to the ground and heard a voice say to him, "Saul, Saul, why do you persecute me?"

—Acts 9:3–4

To meet the Messiah in a yes-or-no encounter forces us to examine and to admit what we hold absolute, which is exactly what happened to the rich young ruler long ago. Jesus had—and still has—a disturbing way of putting everything into a different perspective. In his presence we cannot get by with "almost" or "maybe" or "later." A confrontation with Jesus is always a rigorous examination for the "musts" of our life.

—Donald J. Shelby, *Meeting the Messiah*

A Dream and a Ditch

At seventeen I had a demonic encounter in my bedroom. It was 1976.

I was a high school junior living in Avon, South Dakota. My hometown had a population of six hundred people. My family owned the local bank. I was a good student and active in multiple sports and music programs. A bright future waited on the horizon.

I was agnostic in my stance toward Christianity. I had grown up in a local Presbyterian church, which laid an important foundation for my faith. After entering high school, my church attendance became irregular. Church had become a series of uninteresting rituals.

My life began to crumble in my junior year. My closest friends were seniors and leaving soon for college. I was also stumbling unsuccessfully through the uncharted world of high school dating. I anticipated the prospect of becoming friendless and lonely.

That school year other dynamics were at play that led to my conversion. Two friends and their local church began to pray for me. One adult in particular, a woman in the congregation, befriended and prayed for me daily. She prayed that I would encounter Jesus as the Great Reconciler.

And then, the dream. One February evening I was in my basement bedroom studying. Lying on my bed, I fell asleep and began to dream.

In my dream I was wearing the same clothes as when I had been awake. The basement outside my bedroom was completely dark. It was dark in the way that a rural upper-Midwestern community becomes dark in the dead of winter.

I saw a fiery-colored figure walking down the stairs to the basement. It reached the bottom, pivoted left, and walked the length of the basement into my room. It was as real as the computer I am now typing on. The figure extended its hands to grab me.

I awoke, shaken in a way I had never felt before. I was convinced that it had been more than just a dream. From that point on, my life was disrupted. My cynical view of God and doubts about His existence were shattered. The reality of another world had come crashing in on me.

After my demonic encounter, I began to read the New Testament, slowly unveiling the truth about this spiritual, supernatural world. I was experiencing a slow awakening to a God who disrupted the world and made Himself known. The person of Jesus came alive to me in a new way.

In May of that same school year, I asked a young woman to join me for the junior-senior prom. The event occurred on a warm Saturday night. My grandmother loaned me her red Chevrolet, in which I drove my date to the high school gym. As the prom wound down, we agreed to join my classmates at a movie theater twenty miles away in Springfield.

As I drove south on Route 50, my date and I fell asleep. The car began to veer to the right. I awoke to see us hurtling toward a ditch. I jerked the steering wheel so hard that the car tilted up on two wheels, threatening to flip. We jolted to a stop in the opposite ditch facing north.

God had my full attention.

It wasn't my first car-related near-death experience. In 1973, when I was fourteen, I was riding my bicycle and swerved out in front of a car I didn't know was approaching me from behind. The car struck me at fifty miles per hour, and I flew through the air. The driver said I pushed myself off of the car's roof. I struck the asphalt, completely dazed. In that instant I didn't know if I was dead or alive. My legs were badly bruised, but nothing was broken. I spent that summer recovering on crutches.

A year later I attended the funeral of my older sister's classmate after she was killed in a car accident on prom night. Another wake-up call.

After my own accident on prom night, I began to marvel at how fortunate I was. It was an exclamation point punctuating my new spiritual awakening. I was sobered, suddenly keenly aware of the life-and-death drama playing out around us all the time.

That experience led me to accept a weeklong position as a newspaper editor at a North Dakota Bible camp during that summer. I thought that a week of spiritual retreat would help me think through what I believed. During the week I became intrigued by the topic of baptism. I inquired as to its meaning, and one of the camp pastors met with me at the back of the cafeteria. He explained the gospel clearly to me. I was undone. And on July 20, 1976, I surrendered myself to Jesus.

This was my yes-or-no encounter with Jesus. I knew I had to be fully devoted to following Him—whatever that meant. It would require courage at each step—a trusting abandonment to Jesus and a confidence He modeled when He died knowing God would raise Him from the dead.

The loneliness, the determination of praying friends, the demonic encounter, and the near-death experiences all converged in that afternoon conversation at the back of the cafeteria. I was forever changed. My life was disrupted.

Then something interesting happened. I had a revelation simultaneous with my first conversion. Without any formal training or teaching, I knew that churches were meant to work together. The body of Christ was meant to express itself as one.

My small town was home to several diverse churches. Churches in rural South Dakota were often built by various European cultural groups. The Dutch were Reformed; the Germans were Baptists, Lutherans, and Presbyterians; and the Czechs were Catholic.

Within three weeks of my conversion, I brought all of the local youth groups together to ask the question: What could we do together to impact our high school? We decided to sponsor an evening of Christian films. We also started Bible studies on Saturday nights and before school. Before long, 20 percent of the high school was attending the early morning studies. It was a movement of sorts, in miniature.

That became a thread in my life for the next four decades. Wherever I would go—attending the University of South Dakota, working with InterVarsity Christian Fellowship in Sioux Falls and New York City, and then traveling to cities around the globe—helping to unite the body of Christ became my organizing passion.

When the gospel takes ahold of your life, it completely disrupts everything.

What Is the Gospel?

The gospel is the power of God to forgive us and the presence of God to form us into the image of His Son, Jesus.

The gospel in its simplest expression is that Jesus came to earth as God Himself to live the life we were meant to live, and He died the death we should have died. In His crucifixion and resurrection, Jesus put death to death.

The scope of the gospel includes—yet goes far beyond—its impact on us personally. The gospel does disrupt our lives—it affects our decisions about where we live, who we marry, and what kind of work we do. It also disrupts cultures, cities, and civilizations. Jesus is inviting all of us into this yes-or-no encounter.

Jesus came to not only rescue us but also enlist us to become agents in a gospel movement. God has a strategy. The center of His strategy is to change the kingdom of this world into "the kingdom of our Lord and of his Messiah" (Rev. 11:15).

In my personal journey, the gospel has completely disrupted my life and taken me from rural South Dakota to NYC. It has taken me from a culturally divided, monolingual community to a community that speaks one hundred different languages.

The gospel has led me from my Presbyterian roots and brought me into friendship with Pentecostals, Baptists, Lutherans, and everything in between. The gospel has informed how I earn my income, how I raise my children, and how I attempt to help the global poor.

When the gospel disrupts our lives and penetrates our beings, we become concerned with God's concerns—the spiritual emptiness of a vast world, the economic deprivation of billions of people, the racial divide of our cities. We adopt Jesus's concern over a divided church. The gospel infuses meaning into everything we do—every relationship, every career decision, and every place we plant ourselves geographically.

As we study, learn, and live the gospel, our lives should become organized around *five matters*:

The Gospel Matters. The truth of God turns irreligious people into fully devoted followers of Jesus Christ.[1]

Church Unity Matters. Churches uniting across denominational and cultural lines breathe the aroma of belief. Division in the church breeds atheism in the world.

Cities Matter. The story line of the New Testament is about Jesus going to die in Jerusalem, the religious capital of the world, and Paul going to die in Rome, the political capital of the world. Today cities represent the most rapidly changing demographic in world history, with seven thousand people moving into sizable cities every hour. This represents a new San Francisco or a new Singapore birthed every month.

Millennial Leadership Matters. Most spiritual movements are started by leaders under the age of twenty-eight. Attracting millennial leaders to the church and keeping them is crucial to the flourishing of the church.

Movement Matters. Given the exploding needs in the world spiritually, economically, and socially, the status quo is unacceptable. Christianity needs to grow rapidly in difficult places all over the world—particularly in cities. The rapid development of efforts to combat the greatest challenges in our world today—from human trafficking to grinding poverty—is also essential.

When we say yes to Jesus, all of these dynamics should matter profoundly to us. Being abandoned to Jesus means we identify with His passions and strategies.

What Is a Gospel Movement?

For nearly thirty years I have been influenced and shaped by great modern spiritual fathers, including Tim Keller, Ray Bakke, David Bryant, and Bill Hybels. I have been equally shaped by my pastoral colleagues in NYC from a diverse racial and denominational spectrum.

I have been shaped by the way Pentecostals pray, by the way Baptists share their faith, by the way Presbyterians preach, by the way Lutherans and Episcopalians observe the ancient liturgy, and by the way Catholics speak as a moral voice on the great social issues of our day. I have been shaped by the way Coptic and Orthodox Christian leaders persevere in the midst of great suffering and persecution.

I believe a gospel movement is taking place when one or more of the following three dynamics is happening:

- Christianity is growing faster than the general population.
- Christianity is achieving measurable progress against the great social and humanitarian problems of a city or community.
- Christians are increasingly finding themselves in places of cultural influence, and Christianity is penetrating the arenas of cultural influence: morals, aesthetics, and knowledge.

Paul: A Gospel Movement Leader

The gospel disrupted the life of Saul (who became Paul) in approximately AD 35. He was a Pharisee and a zealous persecutor of the church. In his ruthlessness, he captured and imprisoned Christians and sentenced them to death. Saul was the most violent religious bigot of the first century.

In Saul's story in Acts 9, we learn about three critically important dimensions to his conversion—his "three commitments," we might say—in his yes-or-no encounter with Jesus:

He was committed to Jesus. Jesus confronted Saul on that road to Damascus. It was a profoundly personal encounter. Saul's vision of Jesus was transformed from that of a heretical leader of a tiny sect to a cosmic view of the Lord of the church.

He was committed to the priority of the church. Jesus asked Saul the most important question of the New Testament: "Why do you persecute me?" To persecute the church was to persecute

Jesus. Jesus was indistinguishable from his people. Paul would never forget that moment. He would become the greatest champion for church unity in the history of the church. Later in that chapter, Ananias put his hand on Saul's shoulder and uttered the two tenderest words of the New Testament: "Brother Saul." The greatest public enemy of the first-century church had become its newest member.

He was committed to his future calling. Ananias was told that Saul would become a witness "to proclaim my name to the Gentiles and their kings" (Acts 9:15). The king of the Gentiles was Caesar. Caesar lived in Rome. Saul had a date with Rome. That date shaped his understanding of where his life would lead. While Jesus died just outside of Jerusalem, the religious capital of the world, Paul died in Rome, the political capital of the world. The New Testament can be properly understood only from these two city-centric perspectives.

Paul's "three commitments"—to Christ, to the church, and to his city calling—compose core themes in the last twenty chapters of Acts. We are invited to work out these three callings in each of our lives: our commitment to Jesus, to His church, and to our cities is foundational to a disruptive gospel.

The Gospel Ecosystem

Throughout his life, Paul carried out a remarkably fruitful mission that had an impact on the known world, particularly in cities. God is doing today what He was doing in the first century.

In his book *Center Church*, Tim Keller has drawn a diagram to help readers understand how the gospel penetrates a city. He illustrates three concentric circles:

1. *Inner Circle: Contextualized Theological Vision.* The gospel has to make sense in the unique place where it is preached. Paul was masterful in this. He was able to give evidence to God's existence in his preaching about creation in the city square in gentile cities.

2. *Middle Circle: Church Planting and Church Renewal Movements.* New churches are eight times more effective in reaching new people than churches ten years and older. Cities need all kinds of new churches to reach all kinds of diverse people groups.

3. *Outer Circle: Specialized Ministries.* Every city has diverse expressions of the gospel—campus ministries, justice efforts, prayer movements, marketplace initiatives—all driven by and targeted at various affinity groups. The number of diverse expressions can be quite significant. The big idea is that the gospel in any city is only as vibrant as the depth of unity between diverse expressions of the church. In his letter to the Ephesians, Paul writes, "Make every effort to keep the unity of the Spirit through the bond of peace" (Eph. 4:3).[2]

Writing Acts 29 for City Gospel Movements

Paul embodied the following chain of critical understandings regarding cities and gospel movements:

- Cities shape culture.
- Gospel movements shape cities.
- Leaders catalyze gospel movements.

So the first step toward changing an entire culture for Christ is to combine efforts with like-minded leaders in your own city and to motivate and equip one another for an authentic gospel movement. My hope is that as a result of reading this book you will be motivated to become the kind of leader who accelerates the gospel in your city—and that you will join a growing army of like-minded leaders who want to do the same in cities globally.

Saul's three commitments should cause us to evaluate our understanding of how God is at work in our own lives:

1. How radically am I following Jesus?
2. How abandoned am I to the preciousness and the unity of the church?
3. What is my geographic calling?

Paul's life and leadership confirm that God can use one leader to influence the trajectory of global Christianity.

How about you? What has God individually positioned you to do with your unique gifting and calling to impact cities and, through cities, the world?

Take this journey with me to explore God's grand design for your life and leadership.

Let this be your yes to Jesus. And then go invite others to say yes as well.

WHAT THIS CHAPTER TEACHES US:
Disrupting Your City with the Gospel

The gospel disrupts our lives.

Have you had that yes-or-no encounter with Jesus? Has that encounter radically reoriented the way you think about why you were created? What is different about your life as the result of this encounter? How has your life been disrupted? Pause and enumerate how your life is different because of the gospel.

The gospel infuses meaning into our lives.

God is at work in time and history to redeem the world to Himself. He mysteriously allows the unfolding of empires and kingdoms, the rise and fall of leaders. You were born at a specific moment in history for a specific purpose. God has uniquely positioned you to make a difference for the gospel in your context.

God invites us to join what He is doing in cities.

It is a privilege to be alive at this particular moment in human history. Cities around the globe are growing exponentially. The gospel is permeating these new places just as exponentially. God has a grander purpose for our lives and in one way or another wants to connect us to His purpose in cities. If we are to connect to God's work to reach the greatest number of people in our lifetimes, our work must be connected to cities.

A Prayer

Jesus,

We give You permission to completely disrupt our lives in concert with Your greater purposes. We pray that You will give us the courage to be fully available to You. Teach us what we need to know, tell us where we need to go, and show us whom to join in this journey toward greater consequence in life.

We pray this for Your sake, for love of the great global cities of the world.

2

NEW YORK CITY DISRUPTED

After they prayed, the place where they were meeting was
shaken. And they were all filled with the Holy Spirit and
spoke the word of God boldly.

—Acts 4:31

W*hat challenge in your city is so great that only an intervention by God can address it? In 1984, NYC was violent,
bankrupt, and underchurched. God had to step in.*

City Aflame

My wife, Marya, and I arrived in NYC with a van full of possessions in June 1984. We'd only been there six months when,

on December 22, Bernard Goetz shot four unarmed African American men on a subway train. That incident sparked a decade of racial violence that culminated in 1994 with 2,400 murders in the city.

An entire year was marked by almost eight murders a day. Whites were killing blacks. Blacks were killing whites. Arabs were killing Jews. So much death plagued the city that the morgues ran out of room. One day at the Laundromat, Marya was mugged while holding our laundry and managing three small children. It was a scary time to live in NYC.

One fall night in 1988, we were lying in bed when we heard what sounded like a firecracker. We later learned that a woman had been murdered nearby in a drug-related shooting. She and her husband were showing their son the condominium they were purchasing for him and his fiancée. Ten days later Marya pulled into our tiny driveway after working the night shift at the hospital. Her eyes met those of a man who fit the murderer's description standing a few feet from our home. But he disappeared without incident. We exhaled.

The violence epidemic was not unique to NYC. On Wednesday, April 29, 1992, Los Angeles exploded in violent riots after the announcement of the Rodney King verdict. King was a taxi driver who gained national attention after being beaten by Los Angeles police officers following a high-speed car chase in March 1991. The officers who had beaten King, an African American, were exonerated in court, sparking national debate about police treatment of minorities.

Flames rose from the city for six days. I remember that same week in NYC. On Friday, May 1, as I rode the subway from my home in Flushing, Queens, to the Bronx for a Concert of Prayer, the city was in full panic. Commuters were anxious to escape

Manhattan, and many of the city's stores were boarded up. The agitation was palpable.

What do you do when your city or community is experiencing these kinds of crises? Since 2015, Ferguson and Staten Island have become household names in relation to high-profile racial incidents in the United States. And Baltimore and Charleston have been at the forefront of daily newscasts.

Desperate Prayer for Desperate Times

My mother-in-law, June Johnson, gave me a book a year before my wedding. Simply titled *Prayer*, it was published in 1931 by the Norwegian Lutheran pastor O. Hallesby. In the book, Hallesby reduces the definition of prayer to one word: *helplessness*. That was what we were experiencing in NYC in the 1980s and early 1990s.

Think about that word for a minute—*helplessness*. Doesn't that describe what so many of us experience and feel day to day? We feel helpless regarding our personal finances. We feel helpless about family members and their spiritual condition. We feel helpless concerning the enormous challenges of our communities, cities, and global realities. What can one person or church do about ISIS or imploding economies or declining churches?

In April 1987, I heard a story from my friend Rick Richardson, with InterVarsity Christian Fellowship, describing a citywide Concert of Prayer gathering in Moody Church in Chicago. On a Friday night, one thousand people came together from all racial and denominational lines to pray for their city. African American, Hispanic, Asian, and Caucasian leaders met together.

Pentecostals and Baptists. Methodists and Lutherans. It was a glorious sign of hope.

That June I met for the first time with Ted Gandy and Aida Force with Here's Life (a ministry of Campus Crusade, now Cru). I was working for InterVarsity on college campuses in NYC. Here's Life had developed a strong church network from their "I Found It" campaign in 1976. Force, Gandy, and I agreed to have our first Concert of Prayer in my home church, First Baptist Church of Flushing, on February 5, 1988. The goal was to invite sixteen churches to come pray together.

David Bryant was invited to lead the meeting. God had powerfully used Bryant to rebirth the "concerts of prayer" vision started by Jonathan Edwards in 1747. Edwards's vision was to see Christians "by express agreement . . . come into a visible union."[1] Bryant established Concerts of Prayer International as an organization catalyzing city networks to pray together.

When the night came, we were shocked at the interest. Sixteen churches did participate—*along with an additional fifty-nine*. The diversity of people at the gathering was stunning—African Americans, Caucasians, Hispanics, and Asians, as well as participants from every imaginable church background.

We gathered to cry out to God for our city, our communities, our churches, and our children. David skillfully led us through the event, structuring it around the themes of adoration, awakening, and advancement. That night all those in attendance experienced the power of a well-led prayer gathering. It ended with an altar call for those leaders who felt led to mobilize people for prayer for their region. Dozens came forward.

At our September 1988 follow-up meeting, we concluded the evening by gathering outside an apartment complex's basketball court. We worshiped God together as people looked out their windows. It seemed appropriate that an international community of Christians was standing in unity in a neighborhood where people speak one hundred different languages.

By the spring of 1989, the movement had spread to seven geographic regions of Greater New York.

Pastors' Prayer, April 1990

Our team from InterVarsity and Here's Life decided to have a Pastors' Concert of Prayer in April 1990 at Brooklyn Tabernacle. The church has become famous for its weekly prayer meetings under the leadership of Pastor Jim Cymbala. Prayer and worship permeates this church. We were stunned to see four hundred clergy gather from as far as four hours away. We were now seeing unity among spiritual leaders that we'd already seen between congregations.

Within two years, each of NYC's five boroughs—Brooklyn, Queens, Manhattan, Bronx, and Staten Island—hosted a Pastors' Concert of Prayer.

In January 1992, our team was ready to host our first Pastors' Prayer Summit (PPS). The PPS is a forty-eight-hour gathering of pastors to pray, worship, build relationships, and take Communion together. The model has steadily built momentum over the past twenty-five years. Out of those small beginnings have sprung recent gatherings of up to 350 leaders—the largest annual attendance for any similar event in the nation.

The PPS has been the scene of several dramatic moments, such as reconciliations between pastors who have been separated by years of conflict. In these gatherings, it doesn't matter whether your church has fifty members or five thousand—everyone who comes recognizes that before God we are all part of one body in Christ.

The beauty of spiritual leaders assembling every year to pray is that it creates camaraderie that allows leaders to work together year-round. In the early 1990s, an incredibly important truth was coming to light: the greatest need in any city is not money, space, or programs but *trust between diverse people of faith*. Every relationship has a horse-and-cart dynamic, and the order of these matters. The "horse" in a relationship is trust. If you build enough trust, you can pull any "cart"—any cause, any outreach, any initiative. Praying together builds trust exponentially faster than anything else you can do.

In the past twenty years, trust and pastoral unity in NYC have grown strong enough to pull a number of significant "carts"— the planting of hundreds of new churches (collaborating with Redeemer City to City), training twenty thousand leaders in ten locations (through the Global Leadership Summit), and sponsoring eleven thousand children in conjunction with World Vision trips to East Africa and the Caribbean. The Global Leadership Summit was begun in 1995 by Willow Creek Association to train leaders in an annual gathering in August.

Daily Prayer, February 1995

As the murder rate in NYC peaked in 1994, the church was feeling an incredible sense of helplessness. The body of Christ in NYC was challenged to intensify our prayer beyond the annual gatherings with congregations and pastors. Just as we had been influenced by Jonathan Edwards's model, we began to borrow from another eighteenth-century model—that of Nikolaus von Zinzendorf.

Zinzendorf served as host and spiritual leader for a group of Christian refugees who fled to Germany from Moravia. In 1727, to celebrate their unity, they took Communion together. The Spirit of God fell so powerfully that Zinzendorf challenged the community to apply Isaiah 62:6–7 to themselves: "You who call on the LORD, give yourselves no rest, and give him no rest till he establishes Jerusalem and makes her the praise of the earth." They called their village and their initiative *Herrnhut*, meaning "the Lord's watch."

The Moravians began a nonstop prayer vigil that lasted for one hundred years. From that prayer vigil God raised up three hundred missionaries who launched out in every direction—many to the United States. It's impossible to understand American Protestantism apart from these Moravian beginnings.[2]

Inspired by the Moravians' example, on February 1, 1995, the Lord's Watch was launched as a prayer initiative of Concerts of Prayer along simple lines: thirty churches each adopted one day a month to pray for the city. This little organization, Concerts of Prayer Greater New York, provided a monthly prayer guide focusing on a few basic themes: revival in the church, reconciliation between races and denominations, reforming society, and reaching out with the gospel.

And something dramatic began to happen. The *New York Times* reported that crime had plunged to a thirty-year low.[3] The crime rate continued to plummet *for the next twenty years.* The murder rate dropped from its peak of 2,400 in 1994 to 333 in 2013, an 86 percent drop.[4]

Were other factors at play? Sure. God used updated policing policies and community strategies to bring down the murder rate. Yet Dr. Jeffrey Burkes, a Jewish believer and chief forensic dentist with the New York City Police Department, says, "There is no other explanation for this extraordinary drop in crime apart from divine intervention. There are simply not enough policemen to roam every corridor of every high-rise building in a city of eight million people."[5]

Community Prayer, June 2005

NYC is composed of 176 zip codes spread out over five boroughs. To stimulate deeper engagement between churches and their communities, Concerts of Prayer Greater New York initiated Pray New York! in June 2005. The idea is simple: on the same Saturday every June, each congregation is invited to walk the community surrounding their church—their share of their zip code—and pray for what they see. The point is to motivate congregants to get out of their buildings and into their neighborhoods. As many as eight thousand people have participated in a given year.

The prayer walk from my church in the 11355 zip code takes me and my fellow congregants down Bowne Street, past several six-story apartment buildings and many houses of worship— a Hindu temple, a Jewish center, Korean and Asian churches, house mosques, a Buddhist temple, and a Confucian temple. The Hindu temple on Bowne Street was the first in North America. God really is bringing the nations into the neighborhoods.

A Hopeful Precedent

The last spiritual awakening in NYC took place in 1857–58 after the Fulton Street Revival. The revival began with a prayer effort led by layman Jeremiah Lanphier when he convened six people to pray on September 23, 1857.[6] Within a matter of weeks, thousands of New Yorkers were gathering every day to pray, causing a ripple effect across the nation. Within two years, a million conversions were identified nationally from a US population of thirty million. That's 3 percent of all US citizens joining God's kingdom in just two years.

This prayer awakening preceded the Civil War. Emerging from the Civil War in 1865, another spiritual and social awakening occurred that lasted until 1920. According to church historians, Methodist and Baptist missionaries taught freed slaves to read. This resulted in an African American church that, between 1865 and 1900, was the fastest growing in American church history.[7] Agencies, including the Salvation Army, the Bowery Street Mission, and the Christian and Missionary Alliance, were birthed to bring relief to millions of people suffering in cities. Norris Magnuson has captured the impact of this fifty-five-year period in his book *Salvation in the Slums*.[8]

Is it possible that the global body of Christ is on the cusp of a new multigenerational awakening? The vibrancy of the prayer movement over the past thirty years suggests that this is a strong possibility. The key requirement will be the faithful leadership of many emerging leaders.

What It Takes

I've discovered five principles for any leader to ignite or accelerate a prayer movement in their context:

1. *Discover what is already happening.* It's important not to reinvent someone else's effort. In humility, join what God is already doing—maybe a regular prayer gathering for pastors or leaders. Find agencies in your city that are connecting with diverse ministries and churches. Borrow and adapt from other expressions of united prayer that fit your context, and start with those.

2. *Find a partner.* This might be a leader, church, or agency with a similar burden for united prayer. Once you've found a partner, seek a shared learning experience to grow your understanding of how to initiate a local expression. Research and participate in a National Day of Prayer gathering, a Pastors' Prayer Summit, or a Movement Day event. Come to NYC and see one working model as described in the book.

3. *Build a core group of respected leaders who will endorse your effort.* For the first Concert of Prayer in 1988, our Inter-Varsity and Here's Life team found sixteen pastors who would lend their names and presence to our gathering. We put their photographs in our literature so others could see the diversity of churches participating. We worked hard to communicate our message of unity. And we asked each of these core leaders to bring a strong group to the gathering.

4. *Commit to excellence.* Whenever our team planned something, we worked hard to make sure that the worship component, the facilitation, and the program were carefully thought through. We learned that what sustains any type of gathering over time is its excellence. That will create a hunger in people to return.

5. *Hold to your conviction.* Unity matters—unity in the church breathes the aroma of belief into the world. Disunity in the church breeds atheism in the world.

Toward a Transformed City

After spending thirty years in NYC, I have seen God do "immeasurably more" through the church than what we could have imagined. This is one of the great stories of church history when you consider that Christianity grew 500 percent from 1989 to 2014 in Manhattan, the murder rate dropped 86 percent in twenty years, and we have one of the most united, diverse churches in history. I believe the basis for much of this has been the Spirit of God bringing His people together in our admitted state of helplessness in united prayer. We have entered into the divine mystery with God on behalf of the city we love.

WHAT THIS CHAPTER TEACHES US:

Disunity Disrupted

Disrupting a city's natural disunity requires an informed prayer movement.

We need to become conversant with all of the challenges facing our cities. A praying disciple of Jesus is an informed disciple of Jesus. Awareness leads to knowledge. Knowledge moves us to prayer. Prayer moves us to action.

God can do "immeasurably more" in response to our prayers.

Paul wrote in his letter to the Ephesians that God could exceed our dreams. He saw all of Asia Minor hear the gospel in two years after he preached in the Ephesian town hall of Tyrannus for two years. God is able to do the extraordinary in our cities through a united, believing community.

The speed of the gospel's spread through a city is proportionate to the depth of unity expressed in prayer.

In prayer we acknowledge our helplessness before God and one another. Only God can change the city around us. With our humility and oneness in prayer, God mysteriously chooses to act. He invites us to become the answer to our prayers.

When God gets ready to do something, He always raises up a leader.

Are you that person in your city? Or, if a robust prayer effort for your city or community already exists, can you join? Scripture teaches that God can use one praying person to change the trajectory of a nation, as seen in the lives of Hannah, Samuel, David, Solomon, and Mary.

A Prayer

Jesus,

We long for a fresh, global spiritual awakening led by young, emerging leaders. We pray that You will call these young leaders forth. Empower them with the permission and provision of older leaders. We pray that You would give Your dreams to these younger leaders to expect immeasurably more than we can ask or imagine.

May it be so.

3

THE GOSPEL GROWS IN MANHATTAN

And the Lord added to their number daily those who were being saved.

—Acts 2:47

What would it look like if the number of Christians in your city tripled in size over the next decade? What would that mean for your city's spiritual, moral, and economic climate?

Manhattan in the Mire

The 1970s were traumatic for NYC. The phrase "the Bronx is burning" became popular in 1977 after more than 40 percent of housing in the Bronx was burned to the ground. Landlords were doing what they could to recoup their losses through insurance. Tenants fled the city for the suburbs, masses streaming out via the broadest outlets—the Long Island Expressway and the Grand Central Parkway.

The crack-cocaine epidemic of the 1970s ravaged poorer communities like Harlem, Washington Heights, and the Bronx. According to Harlem pastor Preston Washington, the average income for people living in midtown Manhattan in the 1970s was $300,000, while the average income for Harlem residents was $10,000.[1]

The bleak scenario showed no sign of brightening in the 1980s. Times Square at Forty-Second Street had become a hub for prostitution and pornography. Graffiti was everywhere. Vibrant churches in Manhattan were few and far between.

The birth of the Concerts of Prayer movement in 1988 and the planting of Redeemer Presbyterian Church in 1989 were divinely choreographed. Tim Keller planted Redeemer with a small group of leaders, and in the first five years, the church grew astonishingly to 1,500 members. Keller credits two primary causes:

1. The Presbyterian Church of America mobilized five hundred congregations nationally to pray daily for the planting of Redeemer. This was the PCA's first success at planting a church in a northern US city. Keller says he had never seen anything quite like that prayer emphasis before—or since.

2. The message of grace permeated Redeemer's preaching. Keller spent dozens of hours each week meeting with New Yorkers in the Tramway Diner on the east side of Manhattan to listen and ask questions. Keller's preaching represented

a careful exegesis of the Bible as well as a careful exegesis of the Manhattan culture. His preaching was so effective that it has been described as "flypaper against the culture."

The message of grace also permeates Keller's writing. In his best-seller *Prodigal God*, Keller describes a God who is the real prodigal, a God who is "recklessly extravagant" toward us in sacrificing His Son on our behalf.[2] This view of God has fueled the church-planting movement through Redeemer in NYC and globally.

Redeemer continued to grow in the mid-1990s under the organizational leadership of Dick Kaufmann—a Harvard-trained graduate and gifted church planter. He brought the structure to Redeemer that was necessary for it to grow to 2,800 people by the year 2000.

The new century brought economic stress on the church, with the impact of 9/11 and the subsequent economic crash. Keller was also diagnosed with thyroid cancer. Despite these enormous difficulties, the church grew to 3,600 attendees.[3]

Over the past decade, Redeemer has continued to mature as a congregation. It was able to build its own building on Eighty-Third Street and Amsterdam on the Upper West Side. As of 2015, Redeemer holds eight Sunday services—four at the main campus, two at the Hunter College campus, and two downtown at the Salvation Army campus on West Fourteenth Street in Manhattan. More than five thousand people attend Redeemer every week. Bruce Terrell is giving executive leadership to transition Redeemer from a one-congregation model to a multicongregation model. The plan is to multiply into distinct churches as Keller prepares to step down as senior pastor.

Concurrent with the growth of Redeemer as a church was the birth of Redeemer City to City (CTC) as a missions agency. CTC focuses primarily on catalyzing church planting in major cities globally, as well as distributing Keller's teaching through books and training resources. Keller published fifteen books between the years 2006 and 2015. Redeemer has assisted more than 350 church plants globally.[4]

The Church Multiplication Alliance

A gospel movement was taking root in Manhattan through multiple church-planting efforts in the 1990s. In 1999, Tim Keller, Dick Kauffman, Glen Kleinknecht, and I had breakfast at a Sbarro restaurant. Keller shared his vision to see a movement of church planting. He believed that it would take a community of churches planting different types of churches to reach different types of New Yorkers.

Keller and I decided to begin vision casting in meetings year by year with the dream of starting new churches. Our deep conviction was based on the fact that churches ten years and younger are eight times more effective in reaching new people than are churches ten years and older.[5] As the vision was cast, a community of denominational leaders began to rally around the idea of sharing training and resources to stimulate new churches.

In 2003, I directed the National Leadership Forum at the Manhattan Hilton, in collaboration with Mission America. Keller presented three expositions from the book of Acts. More than a thousand leaders came from cities across the United States. That event galvanized the Church Multiplication Alliance (CMA) into a vibrant entity.

The CMA attracted diverse congregations, including Southern Baptist, Reformed Church of America, Foursquare, Missouri

Synod Lutheran, Assembly of God, Covenant, and Orchard churches. The Alliance benefited Manhattan church planting as well as church planting across all of the metropolitan area. Christianity in the outer boroughs of Queens, the Bronx, and Brooklyn was thriving. In his 2010 research, Tony Carnes, our primary researcher and founder of Values Research Institute, concluded that 15–17 percent of the three boroughs' six million residents are active Christians. Carnes believes that in Brooklyn, two new churches are started every week—primarily within immigrant communities.[6]

Why Manhattan Is So Important Spiritually

Redeemer City to City has written an important summary of why a gospel movement in NYC is globally strategic:

> New York City—the most financially and culturally influential city in the world—also has some of the greatest unmet spiritual and social needs.
>
> A prominent mixture of clergy, non-profit directors and business leaders believe that a vital and flourishing city requires a vibrant and strong spiritual underpinning. These visionaries believe that new churches and trained leaders will bring spiritual, social, and cultural renewal to those who live in and shape the city.
>
> History has shown that great spiritual and social movements birthed in New York City—like its cultural and commercial exports—impact the rest of the nation and the world. . . . Saskia Sassen in her book *The Global City: New York, London, Tokyo* made the case that the great global cities—not nation-states—were the key players in determining the direction of the world's culture. Wayne Meek's book *The First Urban Christians* and Rodney Stark's

The Rise of Christianity convincingly argue that the secret of the Christian missionary movement through the early centuries was that it first won the cities of the Roman Empire. . . .

It takes a movement to reach a city with the gospel. The history and theory of missions tell us that whole cities or cultures can be reached with the gospel. A "tipping point" has been achieved where Christianity begins to have a disproportionate effect on the community's values and beliefs, and the faith grows spontaneously.

Sustained gospel movements like these are never the work of a single leader, church, or burst of ministry activity. They require dynamic church planting movements across a variety of Christian traditions; systems for evangelization and developing indigenous leaders; extraordinary prayer; ministries that help people bring the gospel into their work, and that serve the poor. There needs to be a partnership among all these leaders.[7]

Why Manhattan Is So Important Culturally

NYC is consistently ranked as the first or second most significant global city, alongside London. It is critically important for any person of faith to understand their own city. It is equally important that the global church understand the significance of Manhattan and all of the city.[8]

Jerusalem was cosmically significant to Jesus. In the Gospels, He predicted several times that He would die, and that He would die in Jerusalem. He would launch His mission from Jerusalem, the religious capital of the world—a description the city has retained for three thousand years.

Rome was cosmically significant to Paul. He would go there to further establish the church in Europe, as well as to die. Rome was the political capital of the world.

Modern-day Manhattan is a *financial capital*. More than one trillion dollars is traded over the phone lines every day from Wall Street. In their book *Why Cities Matter*, authors Stephen Um and Justin Buzzard contend that "the top ten mega regions, home to just 6.5 percent of the world's population, produce 43 percent of the world's economic output. Remarkably, the economic output of a highly developed megacity like NYC eclipses the entire economic output of developing countries like Mexico and India."[9]

Modern-day Manhattan is a *media capital*, home to global media outlets like the *New York Times*, the *Wall Street Journal*, CBS, NBC, and ABC.

Modern-day Manhattan is a *cultural capital*. Fifth Avenue, alongside Central Park, boasts many of the most magnificent museums in the world—the Guggenheim, the Metropolitan Museum of Art, and the Museum of the City of New York. The National September 11 Memorial and Museum are breathtaking.

Modern-day Manhattan is a *population center*. One and a half million residents live in Manhattan, and an additional 1.5 million commuters travel there every day. During the workweek, 250,000 people work in midtown Manhattan *per square mile*. Given the Greater New York metropolitan area with its twenty million residents, one out of every 360 people in the world lives within a fifty-mile-radius circle, with Times Square as the bull's-eye.

E. B. White, in his must-read essay *Here Is New York*, sums up Manhattan this way: "New York is the concentrate of art and commerce and sport and religion and entertainment and finance, bringing to a single compact arena the gladiator, the evangelist, the promoter, the actor, the trader and the merchant. It carries on its lapel the unexpungeable odor of the long past, so that no matter where you sit in New York you feel the vibrations of great times and tall deeds, of queer people and events and undertakings."[10]

It has been aptly said that native New Yorkers give the city its solidity, the commuters give the city its velocity, and the immigrants give the city its dreams.

The 2009 and 2014 Research Results

During the peak of the 2008 financial crisis, our teams at the New York City Leadership Center and Redeemer City to City commissioned research to measure the progress of the CMA. We were stunned by the results.

The research done by Tony Carnes and his team at Values Research Institute indicated that the percentage of people worshiping in evangelical Christian churches grew from less than 1 percent to 3 percent in twenty years. They also determined that one evangelical church existed for every 5,853 residents.

Chronologically, the evangelical churches present in 2009 were founded:

Before 1949   25%
1950–1977   15%
1978–1999   19%
2000–2009   39%[11]

Follow-up research in 2014 indicated an additional discovery of fifty net new churches. This grew the presence of evangelical Christians in Manhattan from 3 percent to more than 5 percent. That represents 500 percent growth in twenty-five years. As Tim Keller has stated, "Our goal is to reach 10 percent. We may not reach it in our lifetime but that is the goal."[12] We believe that reaching this goal will represent a historic achievement in the evangelization of the most globally significant community in the world.

The question has to be raised: Why did it take twenty years to grow from 1 percent to 3 percent and only five years to grow from 3 percent to 5 percent? Many factors were at play, including immigration patterns, economic recovery of the city, and increased safety. I am convinced that one of the important factors is the increasingly prevalent expressions of unity in the gathering of Christian leaders from across Manhattan and throughout the entire city. In 2010, Movement Day was birthed in Manhattan, which has annually gathered hundreds of NYC leaders and guests from around the globe. Leaders stimulate leaders. Leaders stimulate innovation.

Leaders have been gathering annually since 1992 to pray at the Pastors' Prayer Summits. Two thousand leaders have been gathering every year since 2005 for the Global Leadership Summit in August. Now leaders are gathering for Movement Day each October. Emerging from the 2012 Movement Day event, CityServe and CityFest began to gather leaders at a local level even more regularly.

The big idea is this: *As leaders are increasingly present to one another, God is increasingly present to the city.* God's presence is what distinguishes Christianity from every other major world religion. Leaders being physically together fosters the kind of unity in which God's presence is more palpably experienced. The vibrancy of the gospel in a city is proportionate to the depth of relationship between Christian leaders in that same city. As the unity of the church deepens in a city, so grows the vibrancy of the gospel in that same city.

The core of the gospel movement in Manhattan can be seen in three great themes: united prayer, effective preaching on grace to enhance the planting and growth of churches, and developing millennial leaders to grow movement.

WHAT THIS CHAPTER TEACHES US:
Manhattan Disrupted

Manhattan matters.

It is important for us to gain an understanding of the great global cities of the world, starting with New York—and Manhattan in particular. Manhattan has become a living demonstration of God at work through a gospel movement, presenting a multitude of dynamic expressions for us to study and experience. Global citizens would do well to avail themselves of this learning opportunity.

Your city matters.

Regardless of where you are from, you need to understand the history, demography, and spiritual landscape of your own city. You need to understand how culture is shaped and the role your city and its institutions play in that shaping. This understanding will inform your praying (chapter 2) and collaborating. Observing the faithfulness of men, women, and churches down through the generations will motivate your present-day activism.

The growth of Christianity matters.

We should all long to see the numeric growth of Christianity in our cities. We worship a God who longs that none should perish. We need to enter into the discontent of Jesus for all people everywhere who need a Savior.

A Prayer

Jesus,

We pray that You would manifest Your Presence in every inch of Manhattan, and especially to the millennials who live, dream, and despair there. We pray that Your Spirit would be poured out into every instrument of influence across Manhattan. We pray that You would heal the brokenhearted and the poverty-stricken. We pray that hundreds of new churches would innovatively be planted to preach the gospel of grace so that all might be drawn to You, the Savior of the city.

Please let it be.

4

MOVEMENT DAY

TOWARD MISSIONAL UNITY

All the believers were together and had everything in common

—Acts 2:44

W*hat is the purpose for which you were born? What is a cause for which you would be willing to die? The answer to these two questions should be the same. There is no greater purpose than to serve instrumentally in helping the body of Christ give witness through its visible unity.*

A Movement Multiplied

In 2009, seven leaders from Redeemer City to City, the New York City Leadership Center, and Concerts of Prayer Greater New

York sat in a Manhattan boardroom to review the 2009 research from the Values Research Institute discussed in chapter 3. The research indicated that Christianity in Manhattan had grown 300 percent between 1989 and 2009. We were stunned.

That same team felt we needed to meet and share with city leaders what God was doing in cities around the world. We decided to schedule the first such gathering for September 2010. Tim Keller agreed to speak, along with Pastor Bill Hybels and Dr. Brenda Salter McNeil. We decided to call it *Movement Day*.

Movement Day became the convergence of two rivers of influence—the prayer movement and the church-planting movement—from the previous twenty-five years. It became an opportunity for the visible expression of Christian unity to impact cities.

Movement Day recognizes a spiritual chain reaction: cities shape culture, gospel movements shape cities, and leaders catalyze movements.

What would we choose as the macrothemes of Movement Day?

Cities. Gospel. Movement.

We wanted to drive a stake in the ground and proclaim the importance of understanding *cities*. We wanted to make sure that our message was *gospel*-centric—we worship a Savior who is impacting the world primarily through cities. We believe in the power and necessity of *movement*; the status quo is unacceptable.

I remember that first Movement Day gathering at Calvary Baptist Church on Fifty-Seventh Street and Seventh Avenue on September 30, 2010. Calvary was an appropriate place to meet, given its enormous contribution to Christianity in Manhattan. Pastor David Epstein was the perfect first host. He has always conveyed a great deal of warmth to the broader body of Christ.

Several ministry leaders had been meeting there for a decade to pray on the first Thursday of every month.

New York City was experiencing a typical September rainstorm that day. As we prepared to open the doors, we were nervous that leaders would have to stand in the rain before they could register in the small foyer.

Remarkably, the rain stopped as leaders lined up around the block to register. It was a thrilling sight. We had anticipated that the gathering would consist of 70 percent New Yorkers and 30 percent outside leaders. It was exactly the opposite: more than five hundred leaders had come from thirty-four states and fourteen countries. Eight hundred leaders attended. For many it was the first gathering that focused entirely on what God was doing in major cities.

The day was structured quite simply. The morning was formatted as a plenary session. Leaders crammed into Calvary's sanctuary—a standing-room-only congregation. Pastor Tim Mercaldo, an important worship leader for the body of Christ for more than three decades, led the worship with his team from Staten Island's Church of the Gateway. Keller spoke about the meaning of gospel movements and why they are so important. Hybels spoke on leadership in movements, reflecting on the story of Josiah, the eight-year-old king who led reforms in Jerusalem. Salter McNeil spoke about crossing racial barriers to foster unity in a city movement.

In the afternoon, leaders joined topical strategy groups on several issues germane to the gospel in cities. We offered this variety because gospel movements are made up of an ecosystem of varied initiatives in a city, ranging from church planting to reaching urban universities to mobilizing marketplace leaders—and everything in between.

What was and is different about Movement Day, compared to almost every other gathering or conference, is our strategy of addressing three fundamental questions within each of our cities:

1. *Where are we today regarding some specific pressing reality in our city?* For example, we in NYC looked and saw that 3 percent of Manhattan residents attended evangelical Christian churches in 2010.

2. *Where do we want to be in ten years regarding that reality?* In Manhattan, we want to see 10 percent of residents attending Christian churches by 2020. We believe that is a tipping point that will result in Christians bringing about greater change.

3. *How do we get there from here?* We need to determine the best strategy to get us from where we are to where we believe God wants us to be.

The big aha in all of this is something quite simple but profoundly important: What our cities need more than anything else is not church planting, prayer movements, or fresh efforts to reach millennial leaders, though these are all urgently important. What our cities need more than anything is a maturing and deepening of relationship between diverse Christian leaders within the same city. Missional unity is the ball game.

It's worth repeating: the vibrancy of the gospel in any city is proportionate to the depth of relationship and visible unity between leaders in that same city.

What are the barriers to unity? To start, there are geographic, theological, denominational, generational, racial, and socioeconomic divides. Yet I believe there is one profound barrier the church has struggled to overcome for two thousand years.

This barrier is what I call the *Samaria Factor*. The Samaria Factor comes into play in any city when churches and communities are geographically close but culturally distant. Ask almost any church leader to describe the ethnic demographic of their congregation. Chances are as high as 90 percent that the leader will say that their congregation is primarily from a particular ethnic background.

In the American context, this is particularly true when you look at the African American/Anglo dynamic, which has developed out of our nation's history. The same dynamic exists between any other given pair of major racial and ethnic groups. Some multiethnic congregations are emerging, but they are the exceptions.

On April 4, 2013, I was invited to host the Manhattan premier of *42*, a movie about the life of Jackie Robinson. Robinson was the first African American to break the color barrier in American professional baseball. The premier date was also the forty-fifth anniversary of the assassination of Martin Luther King Jr. It was remarkable to sit in that theater and hear the cheers of a predominantly African American audience. It sent chills up my spine to consider what Robinson's legacy meant to their urgent need for equality.

Robinson's efforts—along with those of Rosa Parks, Martin Luther King Jr., and others—paved the way for civil rights in America. Slavery had been introduced to North America in 1619. The United States did not pass civil rights legislation until 1965. For seventeen generations, people of African descent did not have basic, decent civil rights. That reality has shaped much of the current demographic reality of our cities.

If we are to see genuine unity, we must respect the axiom that *people can love only that which they know.* Each of us must understand any person who is ethnically different from us in order to love them. This is true between all major ethnic groups in our cities. The essence of the gospel is that Jesus became human in the incarnation. He became one of us. He knew us because He was us.

If we believe that the unity for which Jesus prayed makes the difference in presenting a believable gospel in our cities, then we will need to take seriously the unity gaps in our cities.

Lausanne and Cape Town: Global Unity on Display

The Lausanne Movement was birthed in 1974 in Switzerland when Billy Graham and John Stott convened Christian leaders from nearly every country in the world. The purpose of that gathering was to declare God's passion for the unity of the church and for the evangelization of the world. After that gathering, John Stott wrote the enduring Lausanne Covenant, which is now used by thousands of churches and agencies to summarize their beliefs.[1]

A month after the first Movement Day, I was privileged to join nearly five thousand leaders at the third Lausanne Congress in Cape Town, South Africa. Under the extraordinary leadership of Doug Birdsall, 4,000 delegates from 150 countries gathered in South Africa for ten days to see what God was doing globally to expand world evangelization.

Three seminal moments marked the gathering. First, I had the opportunity to meet Bob Doll—a man globally respected as the most visible Christian stock market commentator. He and I met with leadership from Redeemer City to City so that we might introduce him to our vision for impacting cities. I attended Doll's seminar on the trajectory of global Christianity from 1900 to 2050, which in stunning fashion demonstrated his firm grasp on the world historic picture.[2] In the months ahead, Doll would join Tim Keller and me as the third primary spokesperson for the New York City Movement Project and Movement Day. His understanding of Christianity's global trajectory complemented the work Keller and I had been doing together for twenty years.

The second seminal moment was Tim Keller's talk on cities. He reflected on the story of Jonah and Nineveh, highlighting God's passion for cities and His concern for the cities' inhabitants. This was the most downloaded talk of the Congress.

Third was the Congress's closing ceremony on Sunday night. It was the most celebratory expression of the gospel I had ever seen. The African church led powerful worship. Music and liturgy were woven together into a single expression. Our sharing of Communion with representatives from throughout the global church was an approximation of Revelation's picture of the worshiping universal church. The evening was a celebration of all that God was doing in the world. That experience would weave its way into the future of Movement Day and its global expansion.

The Fruit of Movement Day 2010–2015

As I reflect on the first five years of the Movement Day journey, I would summarize three primary outcomes from Movement Day in NYC.

First, the gospel continues to grow in the city. As mentioned in chapter 2, we have seen Christianity grow from 1 percent of the population in 1989 to 3 percent in 2009, and from 3 percent in 2009 to 5 percent in 2014.

During that 2009–14 period church planters were meeting more frequently as the result of Movement Day and Redeemer City to City church planter training—these were two important contributors to the growth.

Second, the Luis Palau Association (LPA) decided to launch a major CityServe and CityFest initiative in NYC after 2012. Over a three-year period, the LPA team built a coalition of 1,700 bilingual churches (Spanish- and English-speaking) to serve and share the gospel with local communities. Extensive team building has mobilized leaders into grassroots communities. Churches and leaders have begun discovering one another for the first time. In the spring and summer of 2015, these cooperating churches sponsored more than two hundred outreach events throughout NYC. They shared the gospel with more than two hundred thousand people, and early indications are that more than ten thousand people have responded to the gospel.

Third, the vision for Movement Day has taken root in other cities. Movement Day Greater Dallas was birthed in 2014. In the first two years, 3,400 leaders have gathered together. One longtime Dallas resident attending Movement Day Greater Dallas described the 2014 event as "the most significant gathering of leaders I have seen in my lifetime."

In 2017, we plan to launch Movement Day in Columbus, Ohio. A remarkable group of marketplace, pastoral, and mission leaders have been developed under the banner of Catalyst. Catalyst brings leaders together to work on local mission together. Large teams of the city's leaders began to attend Movement Day Greater New York in 2013. Phil Shaffer, Krista Sisterhen, and Scott Mallory have led the charge for Movement Day in Columbus. This is significant, given Columbus's vibrancy as an academic (home of Ohio State University), commercial (lively financial industry), and political (state capital) center.

Other US cities—including Boston, DC, Atlanta, Charlotte, Fort Lauderdale/Miami, and Phoenix—have shown initial interest in replicating Movement Day. Also, Doxa Deo, under the leadership of Alan Platt, hosted a City Changers Movement Day South Africa in April 2015. And other international cities, including Chennai, London (2017), Vancouver, Mexico City, and Toronto, have joined the conversation to explore hosting their own Movement Days.

Leaders from several nations are anticipating Movement Day Global Cities 2016, initiated and planned by the Global City Leadership Community (GCLC). The GCLC was birthed from the 2012 meetings I attended as the catalyst for cities with the Lausanne Movement, along with the Reverend Tom White, founder of Frontline Ministries in Oregon and leader of the most Pastors' Prayer Summits in the world.

The GCLC includes leaders from India, the Philippines, Hungary, South Africa, the United Kingdom, Brazil, Germany, Australia, and the United States. We meet every month, facilitated by Tom White, via video conference to discuss developments in our cities, learn from one another, and pray together. Once a year we meet in person—London in 2014 and Pretoria, South Africa, in 2015. This team has been instrumental in planning Movement Day Global Cities 2016, which is the convergence of Movement Day and the Lausanne Movement.

Our NYC team has had the privilege of making Movement Day presentations to global city leaders—who are enormously hungry to impact their cities—on the Tuesday and Wednesday before each Global Leadership Summit in 2013, 2014, and 2015. We see the Global Leadership Summit and Movement Day as two sides of the same coin, both working to help leaders catalyze gospel movements in their cities.

Over the past six years, several agencies have emerged as important partners in the Movement Day vision: the American Bible Society, the Christian Union, Concerts of Prayer Greater New York, the Lausanne Movement, Cru, the Haggai Institute, InterVarsity Christian Fellowship, the Navigators, the Luis Palau Association, the Nazarene District Office of New York, Prison Fellowship Ministries, World Vision, Youth for Christ, Young Life, the Mission America Coalition, the Denison Forum on Truth and Culture, Duke Divinity School, Frontline Ministries, GoodCities, the Hope Center, and Redeemer City to City.

The Willow Creek Association also has been a significant partner, introducing us to global leaders who want to replicate the vision of Movement Day in their regions. Many of these agencies have been committed to one another, gathering monthly by phone to pray and meeting in person three times a year to pray and plan. This community of partners has provided the backbone of Movement Day. Each of the agencies is an important part of the gospel ecosystem.

How Should You Engage Gatherings like Movement Day?

As you think about what God wants you to do in your city, you may want to take the following steps:

1. Attend a Movement Day experience together with your team to see how it is implemented. Notice the careful thought given to the theme, worship, and plenary sessions. Notice how the afternoon conversations are organized

around leaders who have a passion for a topic, and how a backbone agency provides expertise for each topic. Join the Movement Day Replication Track to discuss specific ways to move your city in this direction.

2. Consider the four critical elements of plotting out a Movement Day:

- Use your best-available research to discover the greatest challenges in your city (for example, church attendance rates, graduation rates, poverty rates, incarceration rates).

- Stimulate ongoing prayer in your city and create a daily prayer expression.

- Identify a core group of churches to participate in the vision.

- Identify a core group of marketplace leaders who want to provide strategy for the development of the vision.

Movement Day Declaration

We celebrate that God the Father is urbanizing the world. The nations of the world are moving into the neighborhoods of our cities. We celebrate that the body of Christ in our cities has a fresh opportunity to reflect a unity that can transform the world.

We confess that we are a divided church. We are divided by race, by denomination, and by geography. We confess that division in the church breeds atheism in the world. We confess that we have yet to fully answer the prayer of Jesus that we be ones whom the world might believe. As Jesus wept over Jerusalem, we weep over the conditions of our cities.

We confess that our cities are broken. We acknowledge that the opportunity gaps between race and class have created an environment that has led to systemic injustice. Our cities are plagued by violence and unrest. This is the consequence of generations of division between class and race compounded by human sin. Sadly, that division is often mirrored in the church in our cities.

We confess that the gospel is urgent and necessary to change our cities. Only the redemptive work of Jesus Christ can rescue individuals and form God's new society as the church to address our broken cities.

We commit to be agents of change. We share a common, holy discontent that our cities are not what God has intended them to be. We commit *ourselves* to be leaders who make every effort to keep the bond of peace in our cities. We ask for the guidance and passion of God's Spirit to know how to act and where we can build trust in our cities—and to create a redemptive difference.

WHAT THIS CHAPTER TEACHES US:
The Twenty-First Century Disrupted

Good research compels action.

We can love only that which we know. The more we know about our community, our church, or our city, the more we will care about its well-being. Research compels us to act. Good research provides the foundation for fostering intelligent collaboration between diverse faith communities.

Vision casting to the city's Christian community is crucial.

Without vision, people perish. Giving expression to what God is doing and can do in our cities is critically important. A gathering like Movement Day helps Christians see God's big picture of their city's physical and spiritual needs and how best to address them.

God is especially passionate about our visible unity.

This lesson is so important that I'm willing to revisit it. The explosion of the church in Acts was in part due to the crossing of cultural barriers. God supports our efforts to bring the body of Christ together in visible, intelligent unity.

A Prayer

Jesus,

You love our city and the church in our city far more than we ever will. We pray that You will give us Your passion to start a gospel movement in our city. Let it start with me. Show me who I should talk to. Show me what You are already doing. Give the church in my city the ability to aggregate our best practices and leaders to make a more significant impact in our city for Your sake.

Amen.

5

THE GOSPEL
IN THE STREETS
OF NYC

The disciples, as each one was able, decided to provide
help for the brothers and sisters living in Judea. This they
did, sending their gift to the elders by Barnabas and Saul.

—Acts 11:29–30

*W*hat does it mean to seek the welfare of your city in a practical way? Are you committed to meeting the physical needs
of your city in a way that makes the gospel attractive to skeptical
outsiders?

God on the Great Lawn

In 1957, Billy Graham, who was just beginning his global career as an evangelist, spoke for one hundred consecutive nights in Madison Square Garden. It was a high-water mark for evangelical Christianity in twentieth-century NYC.

One young twenty-two-year-old Argentine evangelist was inspired by Graham's 1957 crusade and became a protégé of the beloved preacher. His name was Luis Palau. Palau, whose career officially began in 1965, became known globally at the 1974 Lausanne Congress in Switzerland and has preached to more than one billion people in his lifetime.

In a remarkable way, the growth of Christianity in Latin America has paralleled Palau's career from 1965 to 2015. Perhaps more than any other Christian leader, Palau has been the face of the spiritual movement in Latin America. This has been part of a remarkable global demographic shift between 1900 and 2050 (mentioned in chapter 4), in which the world's evangelical population is changing from 78 percent European to an anticipated 71 percent African, Hispanic, and Asian.[1]

The CityFest held in Central Park on July 11, 2015, was the culmination of three years of work by the Luis Palau Association team in New York City, led by Luis's sons Kevin and Andrew. (One of the remarkable achievements of the LPA is its intergenerational leadership team.)

Since 2012, the LPA has recruited 1,700 churches in Greater NYC into a collaborative model of serving their community. Of the 1,700 churches, 700 are from among the city's 2,500 Hispanic churches.

The Palau team, and Luis in particular as a South American, represent the perfect demographic. CityServe and CityFest are clear calls to unity for the sake of sharing the gospel and the relevance of Jesus through collaborative service.

Along with Luis, New York Yankees pitcher Mariano Rivera also spoke at CityFest. He told about how he was transformed from a young boy in a poverty-stricken Panamanian fishing village to one of the great sport icons of the twenty-first century. Rivera emphasized that his athletic ability was a gift from God, given to create opportunity for Rivera to testify about the greatness of God.

NYC Mayor Bill de Blasio delivered a greeting and spoke about the importance of faith and the need for churches to serve communities. He was introduced by Dr. A. R. Bernard, senior pastor of the Christian Cultural Center. The Reverend Gabriel Salguero prayed for Mayor de Blasio in a magnificent prayer that affirmed the need for the church to serve the city and support the mayor in prayer. Mayor de Blasio subsequently told his staff that he welcomed every future opportunity to participate in citywide faith-based celebrations.

How Did We Get Here?

I remember meeting with Kevin Palau in 2003 in my Flushing neighborhood. He was exploring the idea of NYC churches hosting a festival or crusade-type of event with the Luis Palau Association. We sat down in a local Korean restaurant.

I was inspired by the vision but concerned about the strategy. My experience had been that very few national organizations understood the effort it would require to make a lasting impact in New York. Kevin and I agreed that the timing and the model were not quite right.

In 2008, Kevin and his team met with Sam Adams, the mayor of Portland, Oregon. Adams describes the meeting in his foreword to Kevin's 2015 book, *Unlikely*:

> It was 2008. I was a newly elected progressive mayor of a very liberal city. An openly gay mayor at that! Growing up in Oregon, my experience with evangelicals was mostly negative. Based on my direct experience and what the mass media portrayed, I assumed most evangelicals were judgmental, accusatory, closed off, and unwelcoming. . . .
>
> I was weary, yes. Still, I hoped for something different. . . . That meeting went much better than we each thought it would . . . thankfully. . . .
>
> Kevin and the others came with a new kind of offer to help Portland. And their attitude was not at all what I expected. They were humble, not judgmental. They were open, not closed off. They wanted to work together, look beyond our differences, and serve the city. They made it clear they had no hidden agendas. They offered humble community service, not self-promotion or inappropriate proselytizing.
>
> And they delivered. Again. And again.
>
> I so appreciate Kevin Palau and his leadership of the CityServe effort. CityServe Portland has done serious and important work in our city.[2]

The School Partnerships Network, springing out of one Portland-area church's adoption of Roosevelt High School, has become perhaps the most well-known CityServe model in the country. In one year, the graduation rate at Roosevelt jumped from 35 to 54 percent. The progress can be traced to significant investments from both governmental agencies and church-based volunteer efforts.

Here's the story from the Portland CityServe website:

In 2008, Southlake Foursquare Church in West Linn, Oregon, joined a one-day school cleanup event at Roosevelt High School in North Portland. That initial effort awakened the congregation to a long list of unmet needs at the school, including poverty and homelessness among the student body. As a result, the church looked for more ways to get involved, and their efforts grew into an ongoing relationship with the administrators and staff at Roosevelt.

The Southlake congregation has developed a food and clothing closet, a "Summer Nights" community activity program, and ongoing building improvement programs. At football games, church members can be found side by side with students in the stands, sporting Roosevelt sweatshirts donated by a Southlake member as a fundraiser for the school. Though 25 miles separated their campuses, a true "partnership" developed between an inner-city public high school and an affluent, suburban church.

In January of 2012, Portland Public Schools Superintendent Carole Smith learned of this unique relationship between Roosevelt and Southlake. She asked Kevin Palau, President of the Luis Palau Association, what it would take to find "church partners" for each of the schools in her district. Kevin approached a major Christian foundation to see if they would be interested in helping to fund an organized effort. With the foundation's acceptance of the project, funds were made available in February 2012 and a part-time staff was hired to initiate the effort in March 2012. The name "School Partnership Network" was chosen later that month.

What started as a simple inquiry from a school Superintendent has blossomed into a full-scale, united effort to help connect local churches with their area schools throughout the greater metro area. As other school districts and churches have heard about the initiative, they have been quick to jump onboard. A database listing of involved and interested churches is continually growing, meetings with pastors and other community leaders are being held on a regular basis, tools and resources continue to be developed to cultivate these growing relationships, and plans are being made to expand this network ministry throughout the region in 2013 and beyond.[3]

As the CityServe model was rapidly maturing in Portland, Kevin joined several national colleagues in NYC for Movement Day 2010. We met the day before Movement Day with leaders from multiple cities. This was the first point of reengagement for Kevin and me since our meeting in 2003.

Movement Day 2012 and Beyond

Kevin began exploring the possibility of engaging the churches of Greater New York in a CityServe/CityFest model. At Movement Day 2012, my team arranged meetings between strategic Hispanic leaders and the LPA team. In several follow-up meetings over the following few months, the interested parties explored the feasibility of the model for NYC.

In regard to what it took to build out a network to have the kind of impact they sought, Kevin says, "I initially spent three months calling through more than two hundred leaders in the New York City area. I kept telling the Portland story over and over. I wanted to learn what already existed and what churches were doing. It was important to set the right foundation for the work. At the six-month mark, I had met with or spoken with five hundred leaders."[4] This determined effort by Kevin to network leaders was the relational foundation for the CityServe movement.

In the city, the LPA team skillfully built a meaningful relationship with Mayor de Blasio's office. This motivated the mayor to issue a formal endorsement for the CityServe model in NYC. According to the mayor, "CityServe plays a transformative role in New York City. It is helping to fight against the inequalities of our city—neighbor to neighbor and block to block. The faith community serves as a moral leader in our city. Martin Luther King Jr. said, 'Anyone can be great because everyone can serve.'"[5] This is a remarkable statement from a mayor who is a self-proclaimed atheist.

CityServe Metro New York City

CityServe is currently organized in NYC, New Jersey, Connecticut, and Long Island. According to Kevin, "Our team recognizes that this is just the beginning of what can happen in a city. We have only scratched the surface. Yet we believe it's a new day, and leaders are experiencing new levels of unity."[6]

According to New York CityServe's vision statement, it is "a gospel-driven movement that identifies, develops, and nurtures church-connected, neighborhood-focused collaborations through the boroughs of NYC in the areas of justice, mercy, and education."[7]

Expressions of CityServe in its first year included:

- *School partnerships*: growing the number of church-school adoptions
- *Foster care*: equipping and catalyzing churches to care for families doing foster care

- *Marketplace solutions*: focusing on job creation for people living in high-poverty neighborhoods
- *Ministry mapping*: three hundred partners providing information to map the work God is doing in NYC
- *Grants*: one hundred thousand dollars given in total to thirty grassroots initiatives

Leaders in New Jersey are working together to impact Paterson, one of the most challenged urban areas in the country. Jim Bushoven heard about CityServe at Movement Day. He is on the pastoral staff at Hawthorne Gospel Church, a flagship New Jersey church that has empowered Bushoven to give the majority of his time to CityServe New Jersey. According to him, "This has created an opportunity for our suburban church to significantly impact the community in a way that it has never done before."[8]

CityFest Metro New York City

From May to July 2015, 115 gospel proclamation events were held in the city's five boroughs, in Westchester County, on Long Island, and in New Jersey and Connecticut. More than 180,000 people attended, with 10,100 registered commitments to Christian faith. According to Kevin, "Each of the events ranged from two thousand to ten thousand attendees in size. The Latinos had a vision for it initially. They realized that the events had to be bilingual, as their children preferred to speak in English."[9]

CityFest culminated in three high-profile events at the Radio City Music Hall, in Times Square, and in Central Park. Kevin was energized to see the Good News in the City campaign as an expression of CityFest. "There were subway and bus advertisements. Everywhere you looked there was a joyful expression of the gospel taking place in the city."[10]

Thousands gathered at Radio City Music Hall where Christian musicians and artists performed, offering a musical expression of the beauty of the gospel. Palau spoke about "how only on the cross of Christ can you find peace with God." Thousands of people gathered in Times Square to hear Toby Mac and other Christian artists. Jumbotrons surrounded the multitude, boldly displaying declarations of the gospel. Powerful!

The Central Park event was the climax of the campaign. In many respects it was the fulfillment of a twenty-two-year-old Argentine evangelist's dream. God was on the Great Lawn in a powerful way. I looked out from the stage during the prayer for Mayor de Blasio and scanned the great throng against the backdrop of Central Park. It was a breathtaking moment in the spiritual history of NYC.

I asked Kevin to summarize the impact of Movement Day in launching the idea of CityServe and CityFest in New York. He says,

> Movement Day was the seedbed for what happened. People seeing and catching the vision for a city gospel movement. Leaders were beginning to catch a vision for what's possible in a hard place, how this is possible in a place the size of New York City. It took faith to believe it was possible. Movement Day provided the relational network to begin to visit, to form groups, to ask questions. It also created the philosophical framework and relational connection for everything we did. We were also able to plant the seed in [visitors from] other cities to do their own version of CityServe.[11]

WHAT THIS STORY TEACHES US:
Love in Disruptive Action

A city team must lay the necessary spiritual and relational foundation.

In all, Kevin Palau spoke to five hundred leaders to hear their stories and connect the relational dots. This exercise has no shortcut. In many city movements, including fledgling movements, the right person or team has to be identified to do the initial heavy lifting to build out a network.

It always starts with vision and getting leaders in the room together.

It is helpful to start with a vision-casting gathering or event. This allows leaders to be together and hear the same stories. It also creates a common language for leaders to build on, especially across ethnic and denominational divides.

In the context of those initial introductory meetings with leaders, the team must cast a vision and tell stories.

Take full advantage of established and developing movements like those in NYC, Dallas, and Portland. You need to paint a picture of a preferred future.

Most city teams must invest a year in creating the right type of organization for the effort.

That organization has to involve enough dedicated leaders to steward the vision, convene the leadership, and implement the program. For any agency involved, a big part is ensuring that the story of what God is doing is well told. CityServe does an exceptional job of that and has motivated dozens of other cities to start similar journeys.

A Prayer

Jesus,

As the God of compassion and justice, You call us to represent You in our cities. We pray with broken hearts for the great brokenness in our cities—broken schools, broken homes, broken foster care systems. Empower and enable us to make a personal, transformative difference in these difficult arenas. Help us do this with the involvement of the entire body of Christ in each city.

Amen.

6

MOVEMENT DAY
GREATER DALLAS

During the night Paul had a vision of a man of Macedonia standing and begging him, "Come over to Macedonia and help us."

—Acts 16:9

W*hat are you desperate to see God do in your city?*
Have you fully entered into Jesus's discontent regarding the spiritual need, economic poverty, and profound brokenness of local communities?

The Journey toward Dallas: God Is Doing Immeasurably More

In 2005, I was serving as president of Concerts of Prayer Greater New York. The organization was struggling with the fundamental question of how to remain prayer-centric. We had developed several partnerships that were bringing funding for diverse projects, but we were concerned that the soul of the organization—the deep commitment to united prayer—was getting lost amid collaborative programming.

We decided to hire RSI, a consulting organization, to help us figure out the best course of action. Jim Runyan, a senior vice president with RSI with thirty years of experience in development, was assigned to work with us. Runyan helped engineer the New York City Leadership Center, served as board chair of the organization, and then joined full-time to help with the expansion of Movement Day globally.

Runyan, who lives in McKinney, just outside of Dallas, opened the door to several critical relationships in the Dallas area. First was Jeff Warren, the senior pastor of Park Cities Baptist Church (PCBC), a historic North Dallas church. Jeff attended the first Movement Day in NYC and became our first citywide ally for a Dallas movement. Runyan and Warren were our first "men of peace," preparing the way for Movement Day's introduction to Dallas.

Warren hosted a Saturday-morning breakfast in August 2012 at PCBC. Bob Doll (whom I mentioned in chapter 4) spoke at the breakfast. From that meeting emerged a core group of marketplace leaders—Ed Pearce, Bob Anderson, and Dyan Anderson—who were committed to the vision for Movement Day Greater Dallas (MDGD). The group later grew to include Art Alexander, Abigail Powell, Sue Sullins, Tina Jacobson, and Grant Skeldon. This remarkable group has met every week by phone for the past few years to shepherd the development of MDGD.

Starting in 2012, more than fifty leaders per year would journey from Dallas to attend Movement Day in NYC.

Dallas: An Economic Juggernaut

On March 23, 2015, Ray Nixon and I were sitting in a conference room on the thirty-first floor of a downtown Dallas office building on Ross Avenue. It was a sunlit afternoon, and the view was spectacular. Nixon is a leading marketplace Christian in Dallas and a longtime member of Park Cities Presbyterian Church. The view from the thirty-first floor provided a fitting backdrop for our conversation regarding Nixon's optimism concerning Dallas.

Nixon joined Barrow, Hanley, Mewhinney & Strauss in 1994 and has witnessed the firm's phenomenal growth. Now managing more than one hundred billion dollars in assets, the firm provides a fitting metaphor for the meteoric rise of Dallas on the global financial landscape.

Nixon commented, "When the firm began in 1979, most people believed that sophisticated money managers were primarily in New York City or Los Angeles. Dallas was a frontier for financial investment. All of this has changed. Barrow Hanley now does business on five continents."

Greater Dallas has become a financial juggernaut. In Nixon's words,

> The days of Dallas just being about big hair and football are over. It's considered to be the fourth-best city in the country to grow a company [according to CNBC] and the eighth-best city for foreign investment. Dallas is now home to twenty-one of the Forbes Global 2000. Companies are relocating in droves to Greater Dallas—Active Software, the Warren Buffet-owned Van Tuyl car company, AT&T, Toyota's US headquarters, Raytheon, and State Farm Insurance. *MarketWatch* in May 2014 declared Dallas as America's friendliest city for business.[1]

Dallas reflects the attractiveness of its state. In a December 2013 address at a gala at Dallas Baptist University honoring Bob Buford, Governor Greg Abbot reinforced the financial impact of the state, saying, "Texas is now home to seven of the top ten job-producing cities in America."[2]

According to Nixon, "The other contributors to this favorable economic climate are no state taxes, inexpensive labor, and room to grow."[3] As a result, Dallas has become one of the biggest magnets for immigrants in the country. The DFW (Dallas/Fort Worth) International Community Alliance estimates that 44 percent of Dallas citizens, representing 239 language groups, speak English as a second language.

Dallas: A Global City

Dallas is a burgeoning economic engine that has evolved into a cultural, political, educational, and entertainment center on a global scale. Its two major airports serve fifty-six global destinations daily, according to Nixon, with Beijing being the most recently added direct nonstop destination.

"Our professional sports franchises—the Cowboys, the Rangers, the Mavericks, and the Stars—are home to world-class professional talent and attract fans from across the globe. Culturally, we are home to the Dallas Center for Performing Arts—the most expansive cultural center of its type in the world at a cost of $354 million. Dallas is also home to the Perot Museum and the George W. Bush Presidential Library."[4]

Politically, Dallas has been well served by recent mayors Mike Rawlings and Tom Leppert. These two leaders, one a Democrat and one a Republican, have been able to attract significant businesses and political gatherings to the city. Leppert brought the Omni Hotel to downtown Dallas, and Rawlings hosted the annual meeting of the United States Conference of Mayors in 2014. It was the first time the city had hosted the event since 1965. In 2014, Dallas also hosted the New City Summit for eight hundred participants from all over the world in an effort to find ways to improve city infrastructure and urban life.

Dallas is home to some of the finest educational institutions in the world—most notably Southern Methodist University and its Tate Lecture Series and Cox School of Business. SMU recently received forty-five million dollars from the Meadows Foundation—the largest grant in the foundation's history. And the UT Southwestern Medical Center, a medical school established in 1943, has produced six Nobel Peace Prize winners and played a role in developing the statin drugs.

Dallas: A City in Need of Leadership

Jim Denison has been a magnificent voice for the work of MDGD. His website, Denison Forum on Truth and Culture, reaches one hundred thousand daily readers. A vibrant Christian intellectual, he has been described as a modern-day Francis Schaeffer. Denison and his Forum team have provided sobering research on some of the critical needs of the Greater Dallas area:

- **Education.** Forty-two percent of third graders in Dallas County are reading at or above grade level. Only 4 percent of high school seniors read on a twelfth-grade level. Only 1 percent participate in mathematics at a twelfth-grade standard.

- **Hunger.** The number of North Texans seeking help from food pantries or soup kitchens each week has risen 80 percent since 2006—almost sixty-five thousand people a week.

- **Financial stability.** In Dallas County, 29.3 percent of children (more than 190,000) live below the federal income poverty level. Across nine counties in North Texas, the number rises to more than 360,000.

- **Human trafficking.** Twenty-five percent of all international victims in America are in Texas. There are six thousand runaways annually in Dallas with one out of three being lured into sex trafficking within forty-eight hours of leaving home. The average age of entry into sex trafficking is between twelve and thirteen years old.

- **Vulnerable children—fatherless and orphans.** As many as 210 million orphans exist around the world. Sixty percent of the girls become prostitutes, and 70 percent of the boys become hardened criminals.

- **Crime.** Dallas is in the fourth percentile for safety; 94 percent of America's cities are safer. And 223 crimes are committed in Dallas per square mile; the national average is 39.[5]

Like most major global cities, Dallas is a study in stark contrasts along racial and socioeconomic lines. Nixon believes "our greatest needs in our city require effective means of engaging poorer communities that result in sustainable growth. We need a more effective engagement with not only the African American and Hispanic communities but all ethnic communities in the city, and a better creation of opportunity across the board."[6]

Nixon puts his money where his mouth is. His wife, Denise, has served as board chair for Serve West Dallas (SWD), a nationally recognized collaborative in an economically challenged community. Through SWD, agencies have bridged many of their racial and organizational differences to more effectively serve their communities.

Nixon made it clear that Dallas needs an ever-increasing level of statesmanship from Christian marketplace leaders to bridge the economic, social, and spiritual divide between communities.

Dallas Christian Leadership

In regard to the Christian leadership legacy in Dallas, Nixon says, "Dallas Theological Seminary [under the leadership of Dr. Mark Bailey] is a ninety-year-old institution with enormous global impact. Notable leaders like Chuck Swindoll, David Jeremiah, Ramesh Richard, Howard Hendricks, Chip Ingram, and Jim Rayburn have graduated from or served on the faculty of DTS. Rayburn founded Young Life in Dallas, and it has become one of the most impactful movements among young people in the world."[7]

Dallas Baptist University (DBU), a fifty-year-old institution, has more than 5,400 students enrolled on multiple campuses under the skillful leadership of Dr. Gary Cook. DBU offers seventy undergraduate majors, twenty-six master's programs, and two doctoral programs. The PhD in leadership is launching both academicians and practitioners into places of cultural influence.

Another notable person is Ruth Altshuler, whom Nixon calls the city's "grande dame of philanthropy." Her efforts helped to revive the Salvation Army in Dallas, which has now become one of the largest Salvation Army outreaches in the world. Michal Powell is following in Altshuler's footsteps as a powerful force in local philanthropy in her current philanthropic leadership roles. Park Cities Presbyterian members Bob Rowling, founder of TRT Holdings and owner of the Omni Hotel, and Randall Stephenson, chairman and CEO of AT&T, have become models of Christian marketplace leadership, bringing their faith to bear within their spheres of influence. Weir Furniture is another expression of marketplace leadership, with its explicit commitment to function as a company operated by Christian principles. It has had an extraordinary impact in Dallas for sixty-seven years. Also, many senior marketplace leaders have discovered one another on mission trips to Cuba with East-West Ministries, founded by John Maisel, or through working with agencies like His Bridge Builders.

Despite Dallas having perhaps the greatest concentration of Christian marketplace talent and megachurches in the world, division continues along racial lines.

Movement Day Greater Dallas

Against the backdrop of these many relationships, institutions, and enormous challenges, the inaugural MDGD was held in January 2014 at the Kay Bailey Hutchinson Dallas Convention Center and attracted 1,400 leaders. The 2015 event had two thousand registrants.

Each MDGD event has been divided into three parts:

- Morning worship and plenary presentations
- Afternoon tracks discussing areas of passion in Dallas (youth, marketplace outreach, prison reentry, education, hunger, leadership, immigrant care, and orphan care)
- A closing evening session to hear reports and to worship

Plenary speakers have included Tim Keller, Jim Denison, Bryan Carter, Jeff Warren, Matt Chandler, Shelette Stewart, Jon Edmonds, and Bob Doll. Froswa' Booker-Drew from World Vision emceed the first two events.

Leaders who have lived in Dallas most of their lives openly wept at the sight of the body of Christ in all its visible splendor at these gatherings. The events were able to cross racial, economic, generational, denominational, and geographic divides, making them magnificent achievements for the leaders who labored hard and long to see them come to fruition.

Crossing the Racial Divide: Signs of Hope

In 2014, under Nixon's leadership as president of the Dallas Country Club, the first African American member was admitted. The gesture served to highlight the continuing racial divide in Dallas.

Against that backdrop are additional signs of hope. African American leaders like Pastor Bryan Carter of Concord Baptist Church (a predominantly black church in South Dallas that began in 1975) have been intentional about creating conversation around the barrier of race to achieve Christian unity. He and Pastor Jeff Warren at Park Cities Baptist Church (a predominantly white church in North Dallas) exchanged pulpits on Palm Sunday 2015. They continue to work together to erase the racial divide in the city. The relationship between these two leaders was born out of MDGD in 2014, a story that I will relate in greater detail in chapter 8.

Sheila Bailey, the widow of E. K. Bailey of Concord Baptist, is an important leader in Dallas. Bishop Bailey was one of the great preachers in America and a national influence in the Promise

Keepers movement of the 1990s. Sheila leads an organization that ministers to women in Dallas and nationally. She was our primary doorway into Concord, which connected us to Pastor Carter and Jon Edmonds.

Edmonds, an elder at Concord Baptist, has won national awards from Presidents Clinton and Bush for his work in housing in Indianapolis before moving to Dallas. He stepped in as executive director of MDGD in June 2014. Under his leadership, the annual gathering grew 28 percent from 2014 to 2015, with a prominent representation from the African American community.

Froswa' Booker-Drew has been an important catalyst since the inception of MDGD, bringing a large contingency of minority leaders to the gathering. Booker-Drew is a remarkable leader, having served in a national role with World Vision in community development.

The Movement Day 2015 event drew a broad constituency of marketplace leaders, ministry leaders, and pastors, representing more than 175 churches and 525 organizations, businesses, and ministries. Networks, including Unite, under the leadership of Rebecca Walls, have brought diverse communities together. Walls founded Unite, a faith-based network of churches committed to collaborating together. Unite was patterned after Unite in Atlanta.

Walls has been an important spiritual mother to the city. She has exhibited an exceptional passion for spiritual unity, combined with a significant knowledge of the needs of the area. She has also laid an important plank in the foundation of the movement. Walls and I made trips to dozens of gatherings across Dallas over a two-year period to cast vision and mobilize leaders. She has demonstrated a tireless energy to serve the city.

The successful replication of Movement Day in Dallas is a sign of hope for other cities. Leaders from twenty-two states and three countries attended the 2015 event. The remarkable interest and attendance in Dallas has created optimism that leaders from such locales as London, Columbus, Miami, Charlotte, and Boston might reproduce this model in their cities.

Other Fruit of Movement Day Greater Dallas

Several demonstrations of initial fruit are beginning to ripen in Greater Dallas. Some of the fruit is tangible; some is intangible. MDGD has caused the following things to happen:

A prayer movement has been stimulated. In January 2013, six hundred leaders gathered at Park Cities Baptist to pray for the city. Out of that initial meeting, A Prayed for City emerged with dozens of participating congregations. Churches pick one day each month to pray for Dallas, using a prayer guide provided by Unite.

Visible unity has increased dramatically. In a city that is sharply divided by geography, race, and class, Movement Day has brought thousands of leaders together in visible unity. An estimated 40 percent of the audience in 2015 was African American. Significant numbers of Hispanic leaders have also participated. Dr. Albert Reyes of Buckner International is at the forefront of inspiring the Hispanic community to become involved.

The organization Initiative has been born. Under the leadership of Grant Skeldon, a first-of-its-kind organization has been created to mobilize two thousand millennials to connect with churches, communities, and strategic initiatives. At present, no other effort like it exists in the United States.

Marketplace and reentry training is beginning. Bob and Dyan Anderson, in collaboration with Prison Fellowship, have launched an early effort to provide skill development for persons reentering the community from the prison system.

An Explore God program was established in fall 2015. Seven hundred churches (including three hundred Awana churches) participated in a collaborative effort to saturate Dallas with the gospel through creative social media, billboards, a coordinated apologetic sermon series, and community discussion groups. It is patterned after the Explore God campaign in Austin, which engages 375 churches and has seen an average annual growth of 10 percent.

Nixon says, "Movement Day Greater Dallas, in its 28 percent growth in one year from 2014 to 2015, has achieved a proof of concept that bodes well for the future. We need to see the body of Christ come together to impact the greatest needs of Dallas and cities globally."[8]

As he and I concluded our conversation, we determined that the view that March day in 2015 from the thirty-first floor provided much-needed perspective. While it revealed a city with great needs, it also reflected a city with great resources, great influence, and great promise.

WHAT THIS STORY TEACHES US:

Dallas Disrupted

Always start with united prayer.

Cities can see an event like Movement Day emerge within a year of making an initial effort in united prayer. This typically starts with a gathering, like a Concert of Prayer, and then an invitation throughout the Christian community to join a prayer effort that is daily and ongoing, with churches adopting one day a month to pray.

Men and women of peace are critical for establishing a launching point for an initiative.

It is important to find and recruit men and women of goodwill in the Christian community who will make time to gather around a vision and adjust their own plans for the greater good. Leaders like those on the MDGD executive team changed their schedules to meet and join a larger vision. Such leaders naturally emerge from vision-casting events.

Vision casting is critical.

Always work to infect others with the greater vision by bringing leaders to events like Movement Day or the Global Leadership Summit. Effective vision-casting events draw on national voices that will attract leaders. We have utilized the voices and influence of leaders like Bill Hybels, Tim Keller, Bob Buford, Floyd Flake, Mayor Wilson Goode, Luis Palau, Brenda Salter McNeil, Frances Hesselbein, and others.

Organize around the passions that already stir the hearts of local leaders.

When we started MDGD, we were committed to letting the event be designed *by* Dallas *for* Dallas. *People own what they design.* The ultimate success in a Movement Day is neither the day itself nor even the measurable progress on important issues. Instead, it's the maturing of the body of Christ into complete unity. As the body of Christ matures in its unity, progress in meeting the great needs of the city will advance simultaneously. At all Movement Day events, this is addressed in the afternoon topical tracks, which attempt to answer three large questions:

- Where are we today on an issue? (This calls for baseline research.)

- Where do we want to be in ten years? (This establishes a goal.)
- How do we get there? (This specifies the strategies for achieving the goal.)

I am absolutely convinced that God has put deep within the hearts of leaders the very passions He wants to see them release and fulfill in their cities.

A Prayer

Jesus,

We pray for Greater Dallas and all of its seven million residents. As Dallas has emerged as a global magnet for the prosperous and the poor, we pray that Your church will grow in its power. We pray that the church will express its unity in ways never seen before in Greater Dallas.

May Your will fill each pastor, missionary, and Christian marketplace leader with a passion to make every effort to maintain unity in the bond of peace. We pray that You would envelop leaders with resources to engage communities that have been disadvantaged for generations.

We pray this for Your glory.

7

MILLENNIAL GOSPEL MOVEMENT IN DALLAS

Then Barnabas went to Tarsus to look for Saul, and when he found him, he brought him to Antioch.

—Acts 11:25–26

The majority of the world's population is under twenty-five years of age. The majority of the world lives in cities. Investing in and impacting millennial leaders is the single most strategic priority to guide the twenty-first-century church. In what ways are you stimulating a movement among millennials in your city?

The Disturbing Trends among Millennials

I was converted to Christianity at seventeen. I entered college at eighteen. I met my life partner at nineteen. We made a lifetime commitment to missions at twenty-one. We were married at twenty-two. We moved to NYC at twenty-five. We had our first child—who is now a millennial—at twenty-six. Within a decade, I made five major decisions that shaped the following forty years of my life: a faith commitment, an education commitment, a marriage commitment, a vocational commitment, and a geographic commitment. Many have done the same, having made all of these major life decisions before the age of thirty.

In chapter 6, I introduced Grant Skeldon, the founder of Initiative in Dallas. Skeldon has unusual cultural agility. His parentage is South African and Mexican. He is able to communicate easily across generations and across ethnic groups. He knows how to navigate both the church world and the diverse neighborhoods of Dallas.

I remember Grant explaining to older Christian leaders the dilemma churches were facing in keeping millennials: "The United States Army will give my generation a gun at the age of eighteen to carry into conflict. In most of the churches where I have been involved, my generation is asked to pass out bulletins. That is the degree of engagement that many churches have with millennials."[1]

In my June–July 2015 tour of India, Dubai, and Singapore, I discovered that every major city faced the same challenge: churches were losing their millennials. David Ro, the Lausanne regional director for East Asia, says, "Seoul has the largest churches in the world. The percentage of young people staying in the church upon adulthood is 3 percent. The disillusionment with church division and scandal has caused millennials to leave the church in record numbers."[2]

A May 2015 CNN article declares, "Millennials Leaving Church in Droves." The article quotes Pew Research, which found that a "survey of 35,000 American adults shows the Christian percentage of the population dropping precipitously to 70.6%. In 2007, the last time Pew conducted a similar survey, 78.4% of American adults called themselves Christian." The fastest-growing religious affiliation in America is "none," at 23 percent—almost equal to the 25 percent who describe themselves as evangelicals.[3]

At a conference in Bangalore, India, in November 2015, Nyack Seminary's executive director for international relations, Elias Dantas, said, "The average age for Christians globally is fifty-five years, for Buddhists it is thirty-two, and for Muslims it is twenty-five."[4]

Regarding why he thinks millennials are leaving the church, he says, "The most profound thing that millennial leaders want is a place to connect. Social media is a by-product of that longing for connection. Young people desperately want a 'third place' to connect, and very few churches provide that space. There is virtually no transition from youth group to a larger church gathering on Sundays. Most young leaders feel lost and disconnected in that space."

Millennials long to be able to connect—mind, heart, and soul—to a purpose. "Millennials are cause driven. The ALS Bucket Challenge was a huge phenomenon among millennials in my network, but it only lasted three weeks. Young adults tend to only jump on causes when they're popular among their friends. Few continue with them when no one's looking."[5]

In 2013, young blogger Marc Yoder wrote "Top 10 Reasons Our Kids Leave Church," based on interviews in Texas. A summary of the blog, which went viral, is that "the American Evangelical church has lost, is losing, and will almost certainly continue to lose OUR YOUTH."[6]

Millennial leaders like Skeldon are looking for ways to meaningfully engage their cities. "Twenty years ago in New York City the culture thought the church was irrelevant. Today the culture thinks the church is simply against everything. The best antidote to this perception is having very visible acts of mercy and justice," says Tim Keller.[7]

According to Skeldon,

> Many leaders in their forties have been challenged by the idea of finding their purpose at halftime. We need to recognize that millenials are internally being challenged by this question before they even choose their major in college. While generations before chose their future and occupation more off of provision, young adults choose their future more off of purpose. They don't want to make a lot of money but not love their job. They're more likely to take a pay cut if it means they get to do something that makes a difference. I believe that young people can be asking the question of purpose and meaning at twenty, not just forty.[8]

Initiative Is Born from Movement Day Greater Dallas

Initiative was birthed in part because of what Skeldon learned from an organization called Breakdown. This involved thirty-eight churches that, over the course of four years, had begun to develop relationships with one another and had taken initial steps to engage their communities. As a Breakdown participant, Skeldon met Dallas city councilmen and, through these relationships, introduced churches in depth to the needs of the cities.

91

Skeldon recruited volunteers to join the movement. He was growing his heart for the city of Dallas.

When I met Skeldon during the 2013 preparations for MDGD, he had just dropped out of college. In October 2013, Skeldon invited me to speak to a group of young adults he'd organized in Irving, Texas. At that meeting, I cast a vision for what a movement of the gospel could look like among young adults in Dallas.

Then, during my November 2013 trip to Dallas, Skeldon organized a citywide gathering at Highland Park Presbyterian Church to officially launch Initiative. More than 150 young adults from thirty-eight churches attended—along with core members of the MDGD team—and received the Initiative call: to engage the city with the passions that God had put into their hearts as millennial leaders.

Skeldon says young adults in their churches were like a dying breed. "I felt called to be like a Paul in my city. Movement Day created a platform that added ten years of momentum. Movement Day stood for the same values. It wasn't just for pastors—it was for leaders of every generation and every church to come together to unite."[9] At the January 2014 launch of MDGD, 281 young adults who signed up identified themselves with Initiative.

In keeping with the joint dream of the MDGD leadership team and Skeldon, our aspiration is to see future MDGD events involve a majority of minorities and a majority of millennials, mirroring the city's current demographic trends.

Initiative Phase 1 (the Gathering): Focusing on the Local Needs of the City

The first phase of Initiative was meant to draw attention to the great needs of Dallas. (See the research on Dallas in chapter 6.)

In its next meeting after MDGD 2014, one hundred young adults came together representing eighty different churches from Baptist, Reformed, and charismatic traditions.

The group's monthly meetings were held in local churches and varied in attendance from two hundred to five hundred people. Meeting topics ranged from addressing the needs of victims of sex trafficking to education to helping refugees. The goal was to inform and motivate millennials and link them with volunteer opportunities. By meeting in local churches, Initiative won over the hearts of local pastors. These monthly events were called the Gathering and provided the backbone for Initiative's ongoing effort to convene millennials to engage the city in collaboration with local churches.

As the interest in and demand for Initiative quickly grew, Skeldon organized a leadership team, composed at first of volunteers. When Initiative was incorporated into its own 501(c)3 and able to raise some seed funding, five team members, plus three interns, stepped up to lead the organization, with Skeldon serving as founder.

Initiative's call to action is compelling, as captured in this May 2015 blog post on its website:

> Dallas is poised to impact the world.
>
> It's always been a recognized city of significance, but at this point, its posture is pivotal. There are a handful of cities that impact facets of American culture. New York City impacts business. Los Angeles impacts media. Washington D.C. impacts politics. Nashville impacts music.
>
> Dallas. *Dallas impacts Church.*
>
> Dallas is the city with a church on every corner, and some of those churches can rival the size of airports. In fact, what is

considered a "small" church in Dallas is considered a huge church anywhere else in America.

Here's why this matters. For as much as the Church is perceived to be irrelevant or behind in the major issues of society, the world is curious about what God's people are doing, together.

Our goal is to change culture by making millennials Christ-loving, city-changing, Church-investing local missionaries. And what a better place to set a new precedent for how the Church is unifying for the good of the gospel despite our differences than Dallas, Texas?

What if when people doubted there's hope in racial reconciliation, they looked to the churches in Dallas and saw a glimpse of hope?

What if when people doubted there's hope in this younger generation, they looked to the churches in Dallas and saw a glimpse of hope?

What if when people doubted there's hope in a better community, they looked to the churches in Dallas and saw a glimpse of hope?

What if seeing something positive made them see something possible?

With enough committed and Kingdom-minded Christ followers, we can change the culture of the Church in Dallas, in hopes of changing the culture of churches in America, in hopes of changing the culture of America altogether.

What would happen if the gospel sincerely transformed the heart and soul of America, the most influential nation in the world? Let's see.[10]

Initiative Phase 2 (Belong): Inviting Unchurched Millennials to Consider Jesus

In 2015, Initiative created an additional type of meeting called Belong, an attractive party environment to which millennial leaders of faith can invite other millennials to develop friendships. The quarterly meetings typically take place in a mansion or large coffee shop.

"We want to inspire millennial Christians to grasp the same vision for unreached young leaders as described in Willow Creek's Just Walk Across the Room series in training people how to share their faith," Skeldon says. "We want to create a safe and attractive place where unchurched young persons can come and build relationships on the road to exploring Christian faith."[11]

Initiative Phase 3 (Harmony): A United Prayer Effort

It became increasingly apparent that a commitment to spiritual unity was the glue that would hold the movement together. Initiative began coordinating quarterly events called Harmony to bring millennial leaders together to pray for one another, the churches, and the city.

At each meeting, six local pastors share three to five minutes of devotional thoughts. After each pastor speaks, three or four hundred gathered millennial leaders pray based on the pastor's theme. Skeldon observed that many pastors have never been publicly prayed for; laying hands on these pastors has created a tremendous depth of connection between leaders. One of the leaders' major prayer themes has been that God would use them to reach lost people. The results have been wonderful. One fruitful consequence of the interaction with diverse pastors was a 2015 trip with thirty pastors to Israel for ten days. Those who traveled to Israel were interested in seeing another part of the world together. All of this has strengthened relationships between churches, millennial leaders, and the city.

Two Years In: Initiative's Greatest Achievements to Date

I asked Skeldon about the fruit of Initiative's new efforts at the two-year mark. He identified three primary achievements:

People's perspective on millennials is beginning to shift. Rather than millennials simply leaving the church, the church has begun to see the potential of these young members and encourage them as future leaders. The biggest fans of Initiative are older adults. Initiative is providing hope in the next generation.

Diverse pastors are being united in sincere relationships. Leaders— some millennial in age, some older—are learning to love one another and are doing things together as friends, as in the group trip to Israel.

Initiative is fostering lifetime commitments to the city. Millennials are beginning to take responsibility for their city, committing themselves to stay in Dallas for the long term to help the city flourish.

Skeldon says, "George Bailey in *It's a Wonderful Life* demonstrated the power of impacting his city, Bedford Falls, over a lifetime. I have that same vision for Initiative in Dallas."[12]

Over the past two years, Initiative has convened 2,000 millennial leaders and has interacted with 150 churches and 200 pastors, including 80 young adult pastors. Cities across the country have asked Initiative to provide coaching and consulting on how to attract millennial leaders and keep them in their churches.

WHAT THIS STORY TEACHES US:
Dallas Millennials Disrupted

Whenever God gets ready to do something, He always raises up a leader.

It is important to identify emerging, motivated leaders in our churches and give them an opportunity to design and lead a strategic effort in the city.

Create some type of citywide platform that millennial leaders can design and lead.

This should be shepherded and empowered by older leaders, but the older leaders should not be in charge.

Create opportunities for millennial leaders to be inspired by their peers at a citywide or national level.

For example, they might attend a leadership gathering like the Global Leadership Summit, Catalyst, or a Movement Day.

A Prayer

Jesus,

We pray for millennial leaders in cities around the world—that You will fill each one of them with a longing to matter. Equip each millennial with a desire to understand the unique dreams and plans You have tailor-designed individually for them. We ask that You form communities and movements of millennials in cities and in connection with Your church. Please do this for the future of the church and our civilization.

Amen.

8

DALLAS, THE GOSPEL, AND RACE

Now in the church at Antioch there were prophets and teachers: Barnabas, Simeon called Niger, Lucius of Cyrene, Manaen (who had been brought up with Herod the tetrarch) and Saul.

—Acts 13:1

H ow has the gospel disrupted your life in relationship to race? If it hasn't, then there is some important work to be done in you. If disunity in the church breeds atheism in the world, racial unity in the church is the bull's-eye toward which God wants to work. God chose a multiracial leadership team in Antioch to guide the early church in its mission to reach the gentile world.

My Racial Journey

My racial journey began in rural South Dakota in the 1960s. I grew up sixteen miles away from an Indian reservation. The closest reservation town to my hometown of Avon was Wagner, which, according to one report, had 80 percent unemployment.

My family has owned a bank for one hundred years. My interaction with Native Americans began while I was a high school clerk in our bank. I found myself questioning whether I could trust a Native American to repay a loan to buy furniture. The decision whether to approve the loan wasn't up to me, of course, but the questions about their trustworthiness were mine.

My mother grew up in rural South Carolina, in Williams- burg County, which is 80 percent African American. During the Civil War, South Carolina had more slaves than people of European ancestry. Sumter, South Carolina, was the location of the war's first conflict. South Carolinian slave owners did not want their way of life disrupted by the overthrow of the slave economy.

Visiting South Carolina growing up, I could sense the two wildly disparate worlds of Caucasians and African Americans. I learned to distrust African Americans as I had learned to dis- trust Native Americans—a dual prejudice. Growing up like most Americans, I was immersed in a community that looked like me. It was natural to distrust those different. Then I moved to NYC in June 1984 and had to confront those prejudices.

Marya and I found a temporary solution to our search for housing by living with her brother Mark for the month of July. But for August we had nowhere to go. There we were, new to the city, Marya was four months pregnant, and we had no place to live. Miraculously, we were invited to stay with the Roderick Caesar family in Hollis, Queens, during August. Bishop Caesar pastored Bethel Gospel Tabernacle. Bethel has been a flagship church in NYC for seventy-five years. Mark had been attending Bethel since his 1982 summer internship at the church.

The Caesars come from West Indian roots, and the church is a mix of African Americans and Caribbean Americans. The Caesar family not only took us into their home but also allowed us to store our possessions in the garage of Roderick's father—Roderick Caesar Sr. We had no idea at the time how incredibly respected the Caesars were in New York City. They became family to us. We felt welcomed into not only their home but also their hearts.

The prejudices I brought to NYC were overcome by the unconditional love of a family quite different from my own. I learned the important truth that the most powerful experience this side of heaven is to be radically loved by someone radically different.

Race in America

I had picked up *Roots* by Alex Haley and was reading it during the summer and early fall of 1990. I found it to be the most well-written book I had ever read. Haley describes the journey of Kunta Kinte from his capture in Africa, across the Middle Passage, and into the American slavery complex. Haley's ability to describe the indescribable experience of Kinte—the torture, separation, and sheer despair of someone in slavery—was breathtaking. I had no historical reference point for understanding this aspect of American history prior to reading *Roots*.

That same fall I attended Trinity Evangelical Divinity School in Deerfield, Illinois, on sabbatical. At the same time, I began a fast in preparation for a campus-wide prayer gathering I would be leading. I was thinking about the book and the impact of slavery on African people and concluded that the suffering the slaves endured was one of the important story lines of human history.

These experiences converged on me as I sat in my car outside a Deerfield grocery store. I found myself weeping uncontrollably for the suffering of the world and, in particular, for communities in NYC that had endured so much poverty and separation.

In my dissertation research in the spring of 1991, I surveyed five hundred Christians from two Caucasian churches and one African American/Caribbean church. I will never forget the answers to one of the questions I asked: "What do you think has been the greatest contribution of the African American community to the broader culture?" I listed several options—science, medicine, legislation, to name a few. The only areas of African American contribution that white Christians could identify were sports and music.

I titled my thesis "The Response of the White Church to the Black Community." As I reflected on the advent of slavery in America in 1619 and the passage of the Civil Rights Act in 1965, I calculated that people of African descent had lived for 346 years, or seventeen generations, in America without civil rights. It is impossible to quantify the impact of that on a community, but we can know for certain that it has created horrific realities.

The two major themes of my paper reflected on the dehumanization of people of African descent and the resulting disadvantages. Those disadvantages have multiplied over the past four centuries. The fight for civil rights for all Americans, regardless of their skin color, was difficult. Martin Luther King Jr.'s "I Have a Dream" speech has been described as the most powerful speech ever captured on film. King spoke in front of the Lincoln Memorial at the National Mall in Washington, DC, on August 28, 1963, one hundred years after President Lincoln's Emancipation Proclamation. His speech galvanized the national conscience concerning inequality and gave President Johnson the moral courage to enact the Civil Rights Act of 1965. But fifty years later, modern-day America is still wrestling with the consequences of a racially fractured society. Cities like Ferguson, Baltimore, and Charleston have become known for their horrific race riots.

As I have reflected on this racial journey for me personally, for New York, and for our nation, I have become convinced that the greatest challenge facing the church in America is the Samaria Factor I described in chapter 4. Samaritans and Jews hated one another, as the Gospels explain, but Jesus confronted this prejudice and gave us His perspective on race in His familiar parable of the Good Samaritan. The Samaritan, not the Jewish religious leaders, cared for the Jewish victim on the road. Bishop Claude Alexander, in reflecting on the story of the Samaritan, says it is always a matter of proximity. The Samaritan *came close* to the wounded person, while the Jewish leaders passed on the other side.[1]

The Samaria Factor is simple: our greatest challenge in cities is to work with other Christian leaders who are geographically close but culturally distant. The amount of effort it takes is extraordinary. The reward from this effort is *extra* extraordinary.

Dallas and Race

While this chapter concentrates primarily on the dynamics between African Americans and Caucasians, it's important to appreciate the amazing diversity of Dallas. The city is home to a huge Mexican population and a rapidly growing number of immigrants from dozens of other countries. Nearly half of the citizens in Dallas proper speak English as a second language.

In February 2013, I was invited to attend a screening of the film *Friendly Captivity*—a documentary about seven Dallas women from diverse racial backgrounds who traveled together to India—at the South Dallas Cultural Center. This remarkable film highlights the disparate cultural perspectives of the women and how they navigated those differences.

At the screening, I met Froswa' Booker-Drew (introduced in chapter 6), who served as national director of community engagement for World Vision. She is a remarkable leader with tremendous spiritual depth, deep relational capacity, and strong academic accomplishments. She has a PhD and has authored multiple books, including her most recent, *Rules of Engagement: Making Connections Last*, which expresses her philosophy of building relationships. After the first MDGD, the MDGD leadership team identified three hundred leaders who had attended as the result of Froswa's influence. She is a remarkable "woman of peace" in the city. I asked her to emcee that first event because she represented the same values—a passion for the city and an ability to build bridges within the community.

As Froswa' and I talked that day at the film screening, I began an important phase of my education about Dallas. She described the community surrounding the cultural center and the three hundred liquor stores in the area. She explained how the valiant efforts of St. Phillip's Episcopal School and Community Center were changing young people for generations. She described the impact of her church, Cornerstone, under the leadership of Pastor Chris Simmons.

The following month, I visited Pastor Chris Simmons, and he gave me a walking tour of his southern sector community. The breadth of his work in the community is remarkable—serving homeless men, providing GED educational resources, and interacting with hundreds of volunteers who come annually to serve the community through the church.

The most heartbreaking thing I learned during the tour was that the incidence of fatherless children in his local community was more than 90 percent. That demographic reality took me back to the sense of feeling overwhelmed that I had experienced in 1990 sitting in my car in Deerfield, weeping uncontrollably.[2]

According to Froswa', the dynamic surrounding fatherlessness among African American children is called the "conception-to-prison pipeline."[3] One can see the natural progression: fatherlessness often leads to poor academic performance, poor academic performance often leads to marginal employment or unemployment, and employment problems can lead to criminal behavior. Fatherlessness is the ground zero of the social crises in American cities.

One of the most sobering data points is that the need for future prison cells in America is often predicted by third-grade reading scores. Students learn how to read in first through third grade, and then read to learn in fourth through twelfth grade. Without an adequate reading foundation, young people have a bleak future.

Wilson Goode, the first African American mayor of Philadelphia, met a grandfather, father, and son in the same prison. As he prepared to leave, the son said to him, "Please give greetings to my son, and tell him that I look forward to meeting him in prison someday."[4]

Goode provides some national perspective on the dynamic of race and incarceration:

- There are more African Americans under correctional control today—in prison or jail, on probation or parole—than were enslaved in 1850, a decade before the Civil War began.
- As of 2004, more African American men were disenfranchised (due to felony disenfranchisement laws) than in 1870.
- A large majority of African American men in some urban areas, like Chicago, have been labeled felons for life. These men are part of a growing undercaste—not class, caste—a group of people who are permanently relegated, by law, to an inferior second-class status.[5]

Currently, 150 inmates are released from prison *every week* and return to Dallas. MDGD has mobilized the faith community to provide initial training for résumé development for newly returned ex-convicts.

Making Every Effort: Pastor Bryan Carter and Pastor Jeff Warren

Pastors Bryan Carter and Jeff Warren met at the first MDGD in 2014. A year later at MDGD 2015, these two men gave a tag-team talk on the urgent need for cross-cultural friendships and racial unity in the church. According to Warren, "In Christ there's no race, there's no black or white, or ethnicity or nationality. This is a global movement [of God's people]."[6]

Bryan Carter pastors Concord Baptist Church (mentioned in chapter 6). His predecessor, Pastor E. K. Bailey, was a "prince of preachers," and even today an annual preaching conference is held in his name at Concord. Carter has commented that Concord was birthed during the height of the "pro-black" movement.

Carter, whose father was a church planter, grew up in Oklahoma City and began attending grade school in 1980. Originally, he felt called to become a bi-vocational pastor, so after high school he attended Oklahoma State University and earned an education degree. Being a teacher would allow Carter to preach on the weekends.

Carter was able to join the staff at Concord full-time. He became Pastor Bailey's chosen successor and stepped into his role as Concord's senior pastor at the age of twenty-nine. It was an enormous assignment.

Regarding his racial journey, Carter says,

> I had the opportunity to interact with white children in my grade school due to the bussing laws of the early 1980s. I grew up in an all-black neighborhood, but I had white friends from school. I also attended a predominantly white college at OSU.
>
> It was challenging. I had to learn to live in two worlds. I had to learn the language of how to interact with white leaders who were significantly different from me but still retain strong ties to the black community. Concord hired its first white staff pastor in 1999 to lead the counseling department. Pastor Bailey's philosophy was that being "pro-black" did not mean being "anti-white." He initiated "roundtable conversations" between Concord and Park Cities Baptist in the 1990s. It gave people an opportunity to describe their unique journeys from a racial and spiritual perspective.[7]

Carter's fellow pastor Jeff Warren grew up in North Carolina. He first served as a youth pastor at Park Cities Baptist before becoming the senior pastor at First Baptist Church in McKinney in North Dallas. Warren was invited to return to Park Cities Baptist as the senior pastor just as Movement Day was emerging as an important annual event in NYC.

In addition to their collaborations at MDGD, the two friends have begun to conduct pastoral roundtables, one of which was sparked in response to the race rioting in Ferguson.

"Pastors are the difference makers in many Texas cities regarding racial tensions," Carter says. "It was in Arlington, after a young African American man was killed, that two pastors stepped in. In McKinney, where a Caucasian police officer sat on an African American young girl, pastors who had come to our roundtable stepped in to defuse the situation."[8]

On Palm Sunday 2015, Carter and Warren exchanged pulpits. Carter preached in predominantly Caucasian Park Cities Baptist, and Warren preached in primarily African American Concord. It was an exchange covered by various news outlets.

According to the *Christian Post*, "The two pastors have developed a strong relationship through their interaction as integral parts of a coalition of approximately 18 Dallas-area pastors from across the city who periodically meet to discuss racial tensions in their communities and ways that the church can begin to help alleviate those issues."[9]

Regarding his experience preaching at Concord, Warren says, "Our identity is found in our love of God. That is what unites us. We have so much more in common [than what separates us]." After the service, everyone expressed a collective "Wow!"[10]

Carter adds,

Movement Day was instrumental in making this happen. It served as a neutral party, brought the right people to the table, and made the pulpit exchange possible. This is a role that cannot be overstated. What we are seeing now with efforts like Operation Blue Shield creating dialogue between the police and churches would not have happened without Movement Day. As we look to the future, our aspiration is that relationships that are being forged will result in action that crosses the socioeconomic and justice divides.[11]

In September 2015, Carter and Warren invited pastoral leaders to a luncheon for sixty-five pastors of varying races. They honored the important biracial pastoral coalition that had emerged in McKinney, which helped the McKinney Police Department defuse the social unrest in the summer of 2015. Warren and Carter cast a vision for one hundred pastors to exchange pulpits with one another on Palm Sunday 2016 to foster deeper relationships between churches, the results of which will eventually have a positive impact on the community.

In a September 2015 interview with Mark Davis, senior pastor at Park Cities Presbyterian Church, I learned that he had been meeting with Vincent Parker, senior pastor from Golden Gate Missionary Baptist Church for five years in yet another instance of cross-boundary unity. Parker had hosted the above-mentioned September 2015 luncheon.

Critical to the citywide conversation has been Jon Edmonds, executive director of MDGD. (Edmonds was introduced in chapter 6.) Edmonds is an elder at Concord and helped me initially persuade Pastor Carter to participate in Movement Day. Edmonds grew up in Indianapolis and was instrumental in integrating a local bowling alley during the 1970s. His passion for unity across racial lines has been an important thread in everything related to MDGD.

MDGD is passionate about planting a thirty-year vision for the city. We believe that integrating this value of unity across races and denominations is crucial to the future health of the city. We anticipate more pulpit exchanges, joint service projects, and dozens of grassroots efforts that will shape the city for generations to come.

If you want to help advance a similar effort in your city, here are some important places to consider starting:

- Visit a church of a different racial background than yours. Introduce yourself as someone interested in learning more about the history and culture of the church.
- Research your city to find out if there are already cross-cultural groups of leaders or churches meeting.
- Outside the church, plunge yourself into another community or a cross-cultural relationship. Commit to journaling what you are learning as a student of the other culture.
- Create a shared experience with leaders from other backgrounds (for example, a joint worship experience, attending a Movement Day together).
- Be a peacemaker. Find a major issue in your city that prevents leaders from crossing the racial divide, and be the person who crosses that divide and invites others to do so with you.

WHAT THIS STORY TEACHES US:
Disruptive Racial Church Unity

Worth repeating: We can love only that which we know.

Making every effort to advance the unity of the church is a high and holy calling. It is important to become a student of the major ethnic groups in your city and create intentional cross-cultural friendships.

Building relationships across racial lines requires great intention and long-term patience.

Showing up to worship with churches and communities different from our own is an important next step in building interracial bridges. We need to ask God to give us great passion to do this.

We need to become "unoffendable" in building unity across racial, geographic, and social divides. It will take years, if not decades, to create a climate in which diverse communities can work together and trust one another. The seeds for the current work of Concord Baptist and Park Cities Baptist were sewn thirty years ago.

Demonstrate courage by creating action points.

The first action point is to intentionally build a relationship with a leader from a different ethnic background. Joint efforts will organically emerge from that relationship.

God is stirring in leaders' hearts, inspiring them to do something. In Dallas, that stirring has manifested itself in sixteen pulpit exchanges on a path to dozens more. These leaders also have a planned day of service in the city. Parallel movements will look different from city to city.

A Prayer

Jesus,

You came as a "mixed-race Savior" as described in Matthew 1. Help us feel and fulfill Your longing for a united body in all its beauty. Give each of us the heart to be a leader who shares Your passion for crossing racial, economic, and justice divides within our communities.

Help us to be thoroughly grounded in the realities of our city and the enormous needs that must be addressed. We pray that the next generations of young boys and girls will have a future brighter than our own. Use us to create a future of justice and equality for all the citizens of our cities.

> *As it is in heaven,*
> *let it be in our cities.*

9

MANILA, THE GOSPEL, AND THE SLUMS

The next day Peter started out with them, and some of the believers from Joppa went along. The following day he arrived in Caesarea. Cornelius was expecting them and had called together his relatives and close friends.

—Acts 10:23–24

How can inter-confessional partnerships influence the multitudes in the margins in your city? Meeting the enormous needs of our nation's poorest citizens requires intelligent collaboration between diverse partners.

The Multitudes in the Margins

I met Corrie DeBoer in January 1998. We were both students of Ray Bakke in his doctor of ministry program at Eastern Baptist Seminary in Philadelphia. I remember DeBoer, a native Filipino who had come to the United States to study, as a soft-spoken woman with a slight build. Little did I anticipate the depth of her passion to impact the masses of Manila, the capital of the Philippines. We had both been invited to study under Bakke.

Corrie met her husband, Stewart, in 1976 when he went to Manila as a retired US military chaplain. He was stunned by the need for quality education among the poor children in the city. In the 1980s, the Philippines had eleven million preschool-age children, but only three million had access to preschool. From this need, Mission Ministries Philippines, Inc. (MMP) was created. MMP's vision was to create a dedicated grassroots social movement empowering local churches to set up, sustain, and expand early childhood centers in the poorest sections of the city. (MMP recognizes a *social movement* as taking place when an advocate casts a vision to large segments of a population, catalyzes a process where collaborators own the shared vision, and facilitates a way to scale a best practice to impact a city.)

In the past thirty years, seven hundred preschools have been established through the leadership of Stewart DeBoer and Chonabelle Domingo, who started as a teacher in the slums and became a social entrepreneur. MMP's method is to partner with existing local churches to set up schools among the poorest of the poor. Several hundred churches have also been planted to house the preschools. The churches become havens of learning for both children and parents. Evangelistic and discipleship ministries are strengthened, and in some cases elementary and high schools are established by partner churches. As a result of the seven hundred schools, thousands of children have already been equipped for a better life.[1]

The impact of MMP in Manila is a remarkable story. I traveled to Manila in 1999 to attend the National Coalition for Urban Transformation, which was cohosted by DeBoer, David Lim, and Father Ben Beltran. Beltran labored for twenty years in Smokey Mountain, the largest garbage dump in the world, where garbage was once piled one hundred feet high. The dump earned its name from the unceasing decay of decomposing waste and garbage fires. Beltran brought imagination and vision to his parish assignment, where he served a squatter community of approximately twenty-five thousand people who survived by scavenging through the dump. Smokey Mountain changed Beltran. "I learned that God is speaking through the poor. We should not think that only theologians understand the Bible. We have not listened to the poor. Just because they are unlettered does not mean that the truths of the Bible cannot be revealed to them."[2]

Beltran was able to partner with the Philippine government to convert Smokey Mountain into a community development project that provided proper housing and jobs for the twenty-five thousand residents. Beltran received numerous awards for his work, including the 1997 World Vision Robert Pierce Award for Leadership, which recognized Beltran as one of the most effective community development organizers in the world. The story of Smokey Mountain's transformation is told in Beltran's book, *Faith and Struggle on Smokey Mountain*.

At the 1999 National Coalition for Urban Transformation event I was also able to meet Father Herb Schneider, DeBoer's professor at a Jesuit university. Schneider, a German American priest, pioneered the creation of a covenant community called Joy of the Lord (*Ligaya ng Panginoon*). This is a community of charismatic Catholics who welcome Protestants and have committed themselves to the work of evangelism and service to the city. Thousands of Manila residents have made a lifetime commitment to follow Jesus through this covenantal community.

Impressions of Manila

The Philippines has an important history. It was established as a Spanish colony in 1565 and remained a colony until 1898. Although it is surrounded by countries like Indonesia, which has the largest Muslim population in the world, the Catholic presence in the Philippines put a stop to the advance of Islam in Southeast Asia. Other nearby countries like Thailand, Vietnam, and Cambodia are religiously rooted in Buddhism. The Methodists were the first wave of Protestant missionaries who went to Manila.

Metro Manila comprises sixteen cities and one municipality. When one visits Manila for the first time, the most overwhelming impression is simply the traffic and the friendly people. On a good day DeBoer can get to her office in ten minutes. On a bad day the traffic can increase her commute to ninety minutes. Yet Filipinos, who rank as one of the happiest people groups in the world, patiently wait and smile at foreigners.[3]

During my 1999 trip, I stayed in a hotel across the street from the US embassy. Every morning I would wake up to see people lined up around the block. Hearts were beating with the hope of procuring a visa to travel to America. More than three million Filipinos are in the United States, and an additional five million work outside the Philippines, primarily in the Middle

East, Asia, and Europe. The average Filipino earns approximately two thousand dollars per year, or 4 percent of the US average income.[4] DeBoer says that 40 percent of Manila's population is poor. The Philippines' greatest export is its people, with three thousand of them traveling out of the country every day.

Manila has an exceptionally high birthrate, and there are more children than the city's families can care for, creating the need for many large orphanages. According to DeBoer, more than five hundred communities across Manila are considered slums, where families live under bridges and in garbage dumps. And the poor and the powerful live side by side. Wealthy gated subdivisions are surrounded by slums.

The question becomes, How do you impact a city that is terribly crowded, congested, and reeling from the consequences of so much poverty? And how do you spiritually influence a population that is susceptible to religious nominalism?

A Transformational Strategy: A Movement of Movements

A Grassroots and Global Movement

DeBoer has been working for more than three decades in two primary spheres of influence. First, she advocates for a grassroots social movement using the Development Appropriate Program curriculum for early childhood education and grassroots church planting. Second, she advocates for a global movement focusing on master's and doctoral programs that provide training in *transformational leadership*, giving leaders the tools they need to engage the poor and address the causes of poverty. She works among the poorest of the poor in Manila's slums, attempting to raise a new generation of leaders directly among Manila's children and by training doctoral students in the graduate school where she works.

DeBoer sees the need to network the body of Christ across all of its diverse expressions locally and globally by training and sending practitioners who will embed themselves in poor communities worldwide. She sees an opportunity to work on a "common grace" strategy, enlisting diverse partners, including those of other confessions, to tackle issues of common concern—poverty, education, job creation, economics, and the environment. For example, it is impossible to operate in a Catholic country like the Philippines and not work through vibrant relationships with Catholic leadership to impact the city.

DeBoer is a member of the Union Church of Manila, an English-speaking, self-supporting evangelical Protestant congregation composed of believers from more than forty-five nationalities that welcomes people of all nations and denominational backgrounds. She also serves on the planning committee for Lausanne's marketplace conference, to be held in Manila in April 2017.

A Preschool-Education and Church-Planting Movement

Starting preschools has been the bull's-eye of DeBoer's work. According to *The Economist*, "Education in most of the developing world is shocking. Half of children in South Asia and a third of those in Africa who complete four years of schooling cannot read properly. In India 60% of six- to 14-year-olds cannot read at the level of a child who has finished two years of schooling."[5]

DeBoer's work has tapped into the core instinct of parents to help their children have a better way of life. I have seen a video clip of slums where DeBoer works. Young fathers spend an entire day collecting scraps of metal and plastic to redeem for three dollars.

Linking the principles of a social movement—training existing institutions to create schools in slums—addresses multiple needs at the same time. The immediate need of literacy is addressed in the preschools and elementary schools. The long-term need for meaningful employment is addressed as young people grow up and graduate from school. They are more employable as a result of this training. All of this fulfills the commitment to a core assumption—that the first thing people need after Jesus is a job.

DeBoer says her most effective denominational partner has been the Foursquare churches. "The Foursquare denomination has trained one hundred preschool teachers in partnership with MMP through the leadership of Jim Hayford and Mars Rodriguez. In turn, as the preschools are established, some become church-planting platforms. [The] Foursquare [work] has become one of the fastest-growing church-planting efforts in the Philippines."[6] The marriage of spiritual entrepreneurship with educational entrepreneurship has produced a powerful engine to advance the social and spiritual welfare of the community.

DeBoer is also fielding interest from leaders in Kenya, India, and Latin America to expand and accelerate the scope of the global preschool movement by emphasizing the use of online training.

MMP's other aspiration is to incubate a job-referral and job-creation movement led by Grace Buado, a trained leader in this field. Low-paying jobs make it extremely difficult for the majority of Filipinos to exist sustainably. One emerging opportunity, led by Elmer Buado and Kent Rush, is a pilot initiative to help Filipinos make bricks using an enzyme that requires no baking as a hardening agent. The current construction boom ensures a demand for this product, promising a more secure income for a large number of the poor. This is an illustration of how entrepreneurism is a pathway out of poverty.

DeBoer envisions creating a social movement of manpower and employment initiatives by partnering with business and social entrepreneurs. "We also want to see current Christian business owners use their enterprises as platforms to evangelize the city. We want to see the Business as Mission [BAM] model adopted countrywide in the Philippines. We want to motivate Christian marketplace leaders to steward their companies to honor God."[7]

DeBoer recently passed the professional body designer course offered by Easecox Group International, a body engineering enterprise advocating for beauty, health, friendship, and wealth. She is pioneering this enterprise according to the BAM model in order to provide financial freedom for missionaries working with the poor; link them with resources, ideas, and business leaders; and fulfill her purpose as salt and light while conducting business.

A Graduate-School Movement in Transformational Leadership

DeBoer has been working to influence seminaries to make their curriculum contextual, holistic, transformational, and pro-poor. The master of arts in transformational urban leadership was conceived by Viv Grigg, DeBoer, and leaders of the Encarnação Alliance, a fraternal association of urban ministry leaders advocating that Christian leaders be equipped to minister holistically among the poor. The master of arts in transformational urban leadership is a field-based program that prepares students to implement spiritual, socioeconomic, political, and environmental change throughout the world. It has sites in Manila, Chennai, Delhi, Kolkata, Bangkok, Nairobi, Rio de Janeiro, and California.

Currently, DeBoer, Bakke, and Natalie Chan, director of the Ray Bakke Center for Urban Transformation in Hong Kong, are facilitating partnerships between Bethel Seminary (where the Center is housed) and Asian Theological Seminary to offer a doctorate in transformational leadership. According to DeBoer, the Ray Bakke Center "equips and strengthens leaders to evangelize and minister effectively in the cities by means of contextual, Christian-based education innovatively delivered through the urban world, with focus in Hong Kong, China, and Asia. It is committed to be a lifelong partner to those leaders, advancing and serving them with ongoing services like teaching, research, consultation, networking, and collaborative opportunities to carry out city transformation projects."[8]

As part of her global networking ministries, DeBoer ministers personally to some street families she met near her home five years ago. She provides friendship and counsel, linking them with resources and ideas for graduating from their life in the streets.

A Prayer and Spirituality Movement

Intercessors for Philippines is an active network that hosts conferences and prayer centers. This initiative has been deeply influenced by the Korean prayer movement and by South Korea's Prayer Mountain phenomenon. In a separate initiative, Leo Armas of Companion with the Poor provides leadership by providing opportunities for poor workers to experience contemplative spirituality.

People are also showing a growing interest in contemplative prayer and spirituality. Increasingly, groups are using the

Lectio Divina method of encountering God, based on deep contemplation and silence before the Lord. Creating a sustainable spirituality is crucial for Christians in a crowded environment, surrounded by extreme poverty.

A Missions Movement

As I stated earlier, three thousand Filipinos, many of them with a strong Christian commitment, go overseas every day looking for work. Many find themselves living in Islamic communities and are eager to share their faith. The Philippine Missions Association supports more than three thousand cross-cultural workers and is training five hundred thousand Filipino evangelicals employed abroad to be kingdom ambassadors. Missions efforts based in the Philippines are especially significant given Islam's growth in recent years in Asia and elsewhere. Philippine Challenge is another ministry that equips and sends hundreds of Filipinos overseas.[9]

Signs of Hope

DeBoer asked her colleague Bishop Noel A. Pantoja to comment on what he sees as the greatest signs of hope in Manila. Pantoja oversees the Philippine Council of Evangelical Churches, which is a thirty-five-thousand-member congregational body. He says,

> Some of the greatest signs of God's working in Manila include: (1) a new and emerging generation of leaders taking up the lead to continue the work of seeing the whole nation discipled; (2) new church plants and discipleship movements starting across the country . . . and (3) the stronger unity of the body of Christ, compared to the last ten years.

121

A greater number of missionaries (conventional and creative) are being sent out in the mission field to reach the unengaged unreached people groups, to see Bible poverty [lack of access to the Bible] ended in many places, and to demonstrate God's love and compassion in new and various ways.[10]

WHAT THIS STORY TEACHES US:

Manila Disrupted

Incarnation is powerful.

The thirty years of work in the midst of slum dwellers done by Corrie DeBoer and her team reminds us that more than one billion people in the world live in urban slums. This enormous reality is heartbreaking—and we are the ones who can change it.

Sustainable spirituality is necessary.

A deep spirituality makes working among the poor possible. The width of our influence for God is in proportion to the depth of our intimacy with God. This is modeled in the Manila story in many different expressions. I saw the diverse practices of prayer in Manila and am deeply appreciative of the groups focusing on intercession and emphasizing contemplation.

Creative education efforts are strategic.

The planting of preschools to plant churches is a story of ingenuity, addressing the longing of parents in poor communities to help their children. It also addresses the human heart's longing to know its Creator. It connects three fundamental needs: to be spiritually alive, to grow intellectually, and to be vocationally viable.

Knowledge and network are essential for effectiveness.

Effectiveness is rooted in knowing what it means to work toward the common-grace realities of your city. To be effective in any urban context, we must know how to navigate the world of the haves and the world of the have-nots. The story of what's happening in the Philippines is one of building trust across diverse religious, socioeconomic, and political communities.

This is a journey with friends.

This chapter is only a small photograph, cropped from the available 360-degree panorama of what God is doing in Manila and made possible by nearly three decades of friendship. DeBoer has pursued her great passion to collaborate across the body of Christ. Our lives have intersected dozens of times in different settings, including the Global City Leadership Community. Every month several of us from GCLC meet by phone from wherever in the world we are to report, plan for future global gatherings, and pray.

The Movement Day Global Cities gathering was also birthed out of many friendships with the hope that many communities of friends will be birthed from a common passion to foster transformative work in cities.

A Prayer

Jesus,

We pray that You would encounter the people of Manila today amid a crowded and congested city. Stoop down to encourage the poor. Breathe on the church to motivate it, in all of its expressions, to be Jesus to the city.

Continue to unite Your people, multiply Your church, and help believers engage the poor with creativity. Provide the economic breakthroughs that will free millions of people from the slavery of poverty.

Multiply workers in the country and launch them to the nations of the earth. Use the joyful demeanor of the Filipino church to make its envoys transformative change agents in the world.

We ask this in unity with all who love this nation in need.

Amen.

10

MUMBAI, THE GOSPEL, AND THE RED-LIGHT DISTRICT

While Paul was waiting for them in Athens, he was greatly distressed to see that the city was full of idols.

—Acts 17:16

N o more important city exists in the world than Mumbai, given its enormous influence over the rest of India. India is the most complex and intensely religious country in the world, with its five thousand years of Hindu culture. How familiar are you with the challenges and opportunities of Mumbai?

Mumbai: The Cultural and Economic Center of India

As my plane was landing at the end of a direct flight from Newark to Mumbai in June 2015, I was struck by the city's extraordinary skyline. Mumbai rises out of the Arabian Sea on the west coast of India, spectacular with its multiple skylines, modern bridges, and teeming streets. The city's 1911 Gateway to India monument was built by the British as a symbol of Mumbai's role as an entry point to the subcontinent. Mumbai has emerged as the financial engine of India, and it is estimated that thirty of the country's sixty-eight billionaires live in the city. A city of twenty-two million residents shapes how a subcontinent of one billion live their lives. Including the metro area's population of twenty-two million, an estimated one out of every 350 people in the world lives in Mumbai.

Mumbai is a city of powerful contrasts. Against the gleam of magnificent skyscrapers, 60 percent of the city's population does not have access to toilets in their own homes. The Dharavi slum boasts a population of approximately one million people— arguably the largest slum in Asia.[1]

One writer describes Mumbai this way:

> Ancient, yet modern, fabulously rich, yet achingly poor, Mumbai is India in microcosm. Once a sultry archipelago of seven islands, and the Raj's brightest jewel, Mumbai was the dowry of Portuguese Princess Infanta Catherine de Braganza, who married Charles II of England in 1661. Today it's a teeming metropolis, commercial hub of an old civilization seeking to find its place in the New World Order.
>
> Forty percent of India's taxes come from this city alone, and half of India's international trade passes through its splendid natural harbor. In fact Mumbai is the very soul of human enterprise.[2]

I first heard about the challenges in Mumbai from longtime colleague Viju Abraham when we started the Bakke graduate program together in 1998. He has been one of the great spiritual fathers in India, along with his brother Raju Abraham, pioneering important work throughout Mumbai and several other cities in India. Abraham started the Mumbai Transformation Network (MTN) in the early 1990s. The purpose of the MTN was initially to unite the Mumbai church to work together. Tom White, a colleague of mine from the United States, was instrumental in the birth of the MTN. (White has traveled the world, leading more than seven hundred Pastors' Prayer Summits on multiple continents.) The MTN impacts a range of enormous needs in the city through church planting and work among the poor, the imprisoned, and the trafficked population.

The Gospel in the Red-Light District

Out of a global community of more than 20 million people trafficked for sex and economic slavery—the majority of them minors—nearly half are in India.[3] Bombay Teen Challenge, an agency with a twenty-five-year presence in Mumbai assisting people caught in sex trafficking, estimates that four hundred thousand people are trafficked in Mumbai alone, making the city one of the human-trafficking capitals of the world.[4]

Bombay Teen Challenge has collaborated with Hard Rock International to create a photo journal titled *The Cage*, which visually tells the story of sex slavery in Mumbai. Vandana Kripalani, who served Bombay Teen Challenge in fund development, offers an overview of trafficking in Mumbai:

Almost all of the women trafficked into the red-light district are from small towns outside of India, from South India, or in the northeast of India. The families that sell their daughters into trafficking are living on sixty-six rupees per day—the equivalent of one US dollar. Most families are at least four people.

A typical sale [price] of these young girls is between seventeen and five hundred US dollars. The younger the girl, the higher the value. A young girl who is a virgin has an even higher value. The family tells the girls that they have found an exciting job for them in the city with the hope of a brighter future—possibly working in a factory.

We have even had men marry women for the purpose of selling their wives into trafficking. The women are typically drugged. Once they get to the brothel, the exchange of ownership from the trafficker to the brothel madam is made.[5]

The trafficker makes a 300 percent profit selling the young girls into brothels. The girls enter a "breaking in" period that typically lasts from six months to two years. They live in an actual cage and are given rations of only food and water as they agree to participate in the sex industry. Once the women's spirits are fully broken, they begin to solicit men on the streets, constantly supervised by their owners. The average woman performs eleven sex acts per day, or approximately four thousand per year, for ten to twelve years.

The women are told they have to pay off their debt—the price for which they were purchased. The only way they can do this is to climb the brothel hierarchy, buying other women and becoming brothel owners. Ninety percent of the women contract a sexually transmitted disease, and 65 percent contract HIV and AIDS.

How does the gospel make a difference in this ocean of misery? Kripalani describes the work of Bombay Teen Challenge:

> Our team has worked very hard for a long season to build relationships with these girls on the street. It took us two years before we could rescue the first girl. Trust building is a long and slow process in this dangerous environment. We meet with women to counsel and pray with them. We also provide free medical services. Even the pimps appreciate our medical services, as we provide free retroviral medicines, which are very expensive to their prostitutes. We have kept a low profile for twenty-five years. In that time period we have rescued 1,200 women and their children.
>
> Bombay Teen Challenge has four homes to provide care for mothers, girls, and boys. They care for 150 people. Their medical clinic sees twenty-five people a day. Bombay Teen Challenge is an important sign of hope—in some respects a drop of mercy in the ocean of need, hopefully to be joined by a tidal wave of compassion by the global church.[6]

The Church of Mumbai

I was impressed that the institutional presence of the church in India dates back to the first century and the apostle Thomas. William Carey brought the gospel to East India in April 1793. Williams College in Mumbai is a Christian University dating back 185 years.

My host on this first trip to Mumbai was Arthur Thangiah, whose doctoral dissertation helped me to get a sense of Mumbai's political and spiritual history. I spoke in Thangiah's congregation of one hundred, which includes many women and children from poverty-stricken backgrounds. The church's services are translated into Hindi and Tamil. According to Thangiah, many of the congregants began to follow Jesus after power encounters (dramatic, visible demonstrations of God's authority over demons). After the service, twenty people came forward for prayer. Prayers were offered for family members, significant health issues, and fertility.

The median age of church attendees in Thangiah's church is thirty-five. The median age for Mumbai citizens is twenty-seven, similar to the global median age. Enormous attention is being paid to the next generation of emerging leaders, particularly in regard to them as future church planters. Redeemer City to City has provided an important influence, training emerging church planters in India and encouraging Indian Christians to make starting new churches a high priority. The nation's urban population is four hundred million people and growing very rapidly. One estimate is that more than one hundred thousand people are migrating every day from rural to urban India.[7]

Thangiah's congregation is typical of the Indian church nationally in regard to its socioeconomic makeup (more rural in origin and non-English-speaking). One estimate is that the ratio of Hindi or local-dialect-speaking churches to English-speaking churches is 25:1, in keeping with the fact that people from the higher classes are not largely reached.[8]

In his research, Thangiah quotes J. N. Manokaran:

> Christianity in India has a history of nearly 2000 years. But the Christian presence and influence is miniscule and largely among the under privileged of the society. Somehow, the gospel has not been presented as a vibrant option to the rich and the thinking intelligentsia of this country. . . . This includes the academicians, artists, media personnel, philosophers, scientists, finance managers, economists, lawyers, politicians, etc. They are seen as

trendsetters in lifestyle, role models in economic sphere, leaders in political opinion and [those who] set agenda for the nation. There is a yearning for Christians to see these people become disciples of our Lord Jesus Christ and lead a "Christ-ward" transformation movement in this nation.[9]

I met for four hours with some of the heroes of the modern Christian movement in Mumbai. In addition to Viju Abraham and Arthur Thangiah, I met in a circle with the leadership of the Mumbai Transformation Network. The group, a mix of experienced leaders and emerging millennial leaders, displayed tremendous energy in planning the 2016 India City Advance. In February 2016, leaders from thirty-four cities participated.

The Gospel to the Professional Class

During my trip to Mumbai, Vandana Kripalani and her parents, Gul and Sheila, hosted me for dinner. Gul has had significant influence in the marketplace in his Christian witness. He has chaired several efforts to reach out to Mumbai and all of India. He has also built a successful seafood export business and has been deeply involved in the work of international diplomacy as an honorary consulate general, interacting with leaders from 105 countries.

I asked Gul about his journey from Hinduism to Christianity. At the age of thirty-eight, he was introduced to Jesus during a trip to Montreal, Canada. Rita, a family friend, invited him to attend a church where they could pray. "As I was being prayed over, I fell into a deep sleep," Gul says. "When I woke up, I was a believer. I had always washed the feet of gurus in my religion of birth. Now in Jesus I met a guru who washed the feet of his disciples." Gul is very open about his faith. He feels the freedom to interact with the prime minister of India, who knows he is a follower of Jesus. His philosophy is simple: "We need to speak with love toward all of the people of India, regardless of their religious backgrounds."[10]

During this trip, I also was introduced to Anand Mahadevan, a journalist in Mumbai and the lead planter for a new church intended to impact the professional class. Mahadevan grew up in Chennai and moved to Mumbai ten years earlier. He began following Jesus in 1993.[11] Mahadevan wrote about his spiritual journey in a 2008 article titled "I, the Convert":

> I was born a Brahmin and the grandson of a priest whom I dearly loved. I am educated and my current professional standing indicates that I am reasonably intelligent. I am also affluent and my income would put me distinctly in the upper middle class bracket. I guess that would make me high-caste, rich and smart. In other words, I am not a tribal, or poor or dim-witted. And yet, I chose to become a follower of Jesus Christ.
>
> The world would call me a convert to Christianity. I have no problems with that, though I see my faith more as a relationship with God through Jesus Christ than as a religion. And for the record, I can truthfully claim that no one financially induced or threatened or deceived me into converting to Christianity.
>
> I am fiercely proud of my national identity as an Indian and I am completely at peace with my cultural identity as a Hindu. I retain the name my parents gave me. My wife, who also shares my faith, continues to go by her Hindu name. We have two children and we have given both distinctly Hindu names. In fact, many of my colleagues and acquaintances who may happen to read this column are likely to be surprised. They have no inkling about my faith, for I generally don't go about announcing it. But if someone

does ask me the reason behind the joy and hope that is ever present in my life, I am always delighted to share it with them.[12]

So why is reaching the professional class with the gospel so difficult, and why does it need to be done strategically? Mahadevan says, "Starting from my parents, I had the perception that Christians were poor, uneducated, and coming only from the rural areas. I started meeting businessmen, none of whom had been influenced by the gospel. The church has grown in numbers but not in influence. We are at the bottom of the influence pyramid."[13]

The professional class and the ultrawealthy have a staggering influence on Indian society. According to the Boston Consulting Group, just 928 households—in a nation of a billion people— own 20 percent of India's private financial wealth.[14]

India's wealth is concentrated at the very narrow top of the pyramid. The number of people who earn the equivalent of 250,000 US dollars is less than 2 percent of the population. Additionally, an extraordinary number of people are pouring into Mumbai.

The city is both the financial and cultural capital of India. Mumbai is where the business community and Bollywood, the movie industry, are interconnected. Perhaps the biggest challenge and most strategic opportunity for the church in India is learning to contextualize among the professional class of Mumbai.[15]

WHAT THIS STORY TEACHES US:

Mumbai Disrupted

Take courage.

I marvel at the leaders of the Indian church in Mumbai who have made incredibly difficult decisions to work in a daunting environment and cross the line of faith. Many have made the extraordinary commitment to work among the poor, the prostitutes, and the prisoners. The gospel challenges us to give everything we have to tell the world about Jesus.

Enter emotionally into the pain of a city.

In a country and city of so many people, the needs can be overwhelming. We must remember the sacredness of every life. We have to find the emotional courage to enter into the suffering of a city and its citizens.

Make wise decisions regarding strategy.

Given the disproportionate influence of the professional class in Mumbai, the global church needs to be alert to the opportunities available at that level to impact the city. We need to ask God for qualified laborers to carry out this work and the resources to accelerate it.

We also need to encourage all efforts to reach millennial leaders in this financial and entertainment center. These young leaders shape the future of the city and the subcontinent.

Prepare to exercise long-suffering and strong faith.

The spiritual fathers and mothers of India have prayed for decades to see some of the opportunities that are beginning to emerge now. Representing a minority religious community causes leaders to look to God for supernatural vision and strength to persevere in one of the most remarkable places in the world.

The church in India is growing, primarily among the poor and outcast. Some unofficial estimates report India's Christian population to be as high as 8 percent. Hundreds of thousands have been rescued from slavery and despair. The vision and hope is that millions more will encounter the living Jesus, who comforts the broken, removes idols from the human heart, and gives meaning to the affluent. May the church in Mumbai be a gateway to a global urban renewal movement.

A Prayer

Jesus,

We pray for this great city Mumbai—the gateway to the subcontinent. May You, Lord, enter through the gateway of many hearts this day. We pray for the troubled and despairing, as well as for the affluent.

May You breathe on Your church across Mumbai. May a new generation of men and women discover You as the fulfillment of all their longings. May You be tender toward the suffering this day and use Your church to fulfill Your beautiful will in the world.

Amen.

11

CHENNAI, THE GOSPEL, AND AN APOSTOLIC CALLING

While they were worshiping the Lord and fasting, the Holy Spirit said, "Set apart for me Barnabas and Saul for the work to which I have called them." So after they had fasted and prayed, they placed their hands on them and sent them off.

—Acts 13:2–3

T he city of Chennai is a cradle of Christianity. The apostle Thomas came to South India and planted the gospel two thousand years ago, initiating one hundred generations of Christianity in this region of the world. Can we link arms with the body of Christ *in this region, which is so uniquely positioned to impact the most densely populated country on the planet?*

Chennai: A First-Century Cradle of the Gospel

I landed in Chennai on June 29, 2015. It was my first time visiting the city. I was greeted by Jeyakaran (Jake) Emmanuel, pastor of Chennai's Powerhouse Church, and Mark Visvasam, who works with a church-planting agency. We had met in Pretoria just the preceding April. I had come in response to Emmanuel and Visvasam's invitation to speak to their Converge gathering.

The trip was serendipitous for me at a personal level, as I met my daughter's future in-laws for the first time. (My daughter's husband came from India to the United States to earn two college degrees and met my daughter at Teach for America. They married in November 2015.)

Emmanuel and Visvasam experienced their first taste of Movement Day in Pretoria and now have a vision to take the same model to Chennai. They recognize significant stirrings across India. Earlier in 2015 was the second national gathering for collaborative prayer and church planting. And the two men were looking forward to gathering in Mumbai with hundreds of Indian Christian leaders in February 2016 to promote unity and collaboration at the India City Advance (mentioned in chapter 10).

On the way to the Converge gathering on June 30, we drove by the grave of the apostle Thomas. Emmanuel and Visvasam reflected, "We believe that given the legacy of Saint Thomas, perhaps Chennai has an apostolic calling as a city. We represent four thousand churches from very diverse backgrounds. Our Christian population is about 15 percent of the total population. We are eager to fulfill our assignment as the 'Antioch' of India to send laborers throughout the nation."[1]

The City of Chennai

Chennai, the fourth-largest city in India, is located on the southeast coast of the country and is home to nearly ten million people. It is the capital of the Tamil Nadu state. Emmanuel and Visvasam described Chennai as the "Detroit of India." The city produces an enormous number of vehicles both for the country and for export. It is also an internet technology hub, boasting the second-largest IT presence in India, after Bangalore.

As an industrious urban center, Chennai has attracted five hundred thousand migrant workers from northern India, three hundred thousand for the IT industry alone. Chennai also has a strategic shipping industry for imports and exports. Companies like Motorola and Samsung have created a huge industrial corridor.

People in Chennai speak Tamil, the language of sixty million people globally. The middle class of India has been the fastest-growing middle class in the world since the year 2000. As we drove through the city, I could tell this was an ancient city, filled with economic and spiritual life—Hindu temples, churches, and mosques in every direction.

Challenges to the Gospel in Chennai

Emmanuel and Visvasam summarized what they thought were the three biggest challenges for the city:

Education for the Poor and Vulnerable

The slum population has been increasing over the past few decades, almost doubling the number of people living in poverty in the past two decades alone. As India's total population increases, so does the slum population. Despite reform efforts and aid, many of those living in the slums do not have access to electricity or clean water.

The slums of Chennai are found in its back alleys, where huts line the dirt streets. A majority of the slums found in large Indian cities are collections of crowded, single-room houses with poor sanitation and unclean drinking water, which ultimately contribute to the spread of disease.

According to Nada Sewidan, an Egyptian author at *Borgen Magazine*, "In 2011, an estimated 29 percent of the population in Chennai were living in the slums of the city, which is less than other parts of India. For example, in 2011 30 to 40 percent of the population living in Mumbai and Kolkota were living in slums."[2]

According to the *Times of India*, Chennai is one of the country's prime spots for human trafficking:

> The arrest of the managing director of the Saravana Bhavan chain of hotels on charges of faking papers to help his employees get US visas is not an isolated case. Chennai is one of the leading human trafficking hub[s] in the country—the key players being scheming travel agents, some business firms which have branches overseas and a section of the entertainment industry which routinely sends people abroad on shooting assignments. All of them cash in on the dreams of youth to work in a foreign land.[3]

In August 2012, Pranitha Timothy, one of the Converge presenters, spoke at the Global Leadership Summit at Willow Creek on the topic of "speaking out" for the poor. She recognized the organizational strength of many nongovernmental organizations in Chennai, including Compassion International, World Vision, International Justice Mission, Prison Fellowship, and Opportunity International. These agencies represent the potential to advance the work among the poor and vulnerable in the spirit of Movement Day and to align multiple agencies for greater aggregate effectiveness.[4]

Employment

According to one report, "The sharpest rise in unemployment among women was seen in Chennai, where the rate rose 17 percentage points—from 2.3 per cent in 2004–05 to 18.8 per cent in 2009–10. This was followed by Ludhiana (14 percentage points). Ludhiana, along with Agra, recorded the highest rise in the unemployment rate among men (five percentage points)."[5]

The higher education levels for women have increased the supply of qualified workers, decreasing job availability and increasing unemployment. This huge metropolitan area has seen mounting insecurity among the growing number of people competing for fewer jobs, including an influx of migrants, a growing upwardly mobile middle class, and more persons with very specific skill sets coming to Chennai.

Environmental Pollution

Pollution in India has become out of control. The concern about pollution being a major cause of illness and death in India is corroborated by this report:

According to this year's Global Burden of Disease estimates, one-fifth of deaths across the world occur from outdoor air pollution. Also, outdoor air pollution is the fifth leading cause of deaths in India. These alarming pieces of information have drawn everyone's attention and forced experts to take stock of pollution trends in India's cities—including Chennai.

A recent analysis of Chennai's air quality, done by Centre for Science and Environment (CSE), the New Delhi-based research and advocacy body, indicates that though Chennai shows deceptively low to moderate pollution levels because of its location near the sea, local impacts and exposure are high and the pollution levels are rising steadily, thereby increasing public health risks.[6]

Converge Conference and Movement Day in Chennai

"Blood, Sweat, and Tears," Emmanuel's opening talk at the Converge event I attended in Chennai, gave a historical overview of the impact of churches in the city. He described the deep sense of indebtedness that the church owed to diverse intercessory groups. For twenty-five years, Pastor D. Mohan, G. P. S. Robinson, and Sam Jebadurai have met with pastors to pray. Tom White from Portland, Oregon (mentioned in chapter 10), led critically important prayer summits in Chennai.

The examples are powerful and widespread. For instance, the National Prayer Network birthed in Chennai conducted seventy-two hours of prayer leading up to each national election. Light Up Chennai, a monthly prayer gathering, has taken place every third Friday for the past thirteen years. And the Global Day of Prayer gathered eighty thousand believers for prayer in the YMCA Nandanam Stadium.

So where did all of this start? Much of it can be attributed to Billy Graham, who deeply influenced Chennai in his 1956 outreach, leading to a revival of evangelism. Many mission agencies were birthed as the result of this effort, including Youth for Christ India, Friends Missionary Prayer Band, and India Evangelical Mission. This led to extraordinary church growth: there are now more than four thousand churches in Chennai.

The gains from the growth of Christianity were solidified by the development of pastors' fellowships. Pastors were inspired by the work of Tim Svoboda from Youth with a Mission and the videos of George Otis Jr. Pastors in Chennai designed a strategy to divide the city into twelve zones and pastors' fellowships. Today Chennai is home to 106 pastors' fellowships.[7]

The Chennai Transformation Network (CTN) is a sister movement to the Mumbai Transformation Network, a group I mentioned earlier that was started by my colleague Viju Abraham. The seeds for the CTN were planted when the city was partitioned into the twelve zones by participating leaders, and it was officially birthed in January 1996. The CTN welcomed laity and professionals, with participants from Pentecostal, evangelical, and Catholic backgrounds.

The CTN's vision is "Serving and transforming Greater Chennai by every means possible through an effective witnessing community in every neighborhood, [all] people groups, and all spheres of society."[8] What makes the efforts of the CTN important is the group's contextual commitment to economic sufficiency, social peace, public justice, and national righteousness.

A future Movement Day in Chennai is planned for up to five thousand leaders. The metropolitan region of ten million people and four thousand churches presents some complex dynamics. Emmanuel and Visvasam both believe that relationships between all of the members of the "gospel ecosystem" need to become more mature to ensure the greatest impact. The ecosystem (mentioned in chapter 1) is composed of churches, pastors, nonprofit leaders, marketplace leaders, and diverse nonprofit agencies. The vibrancy of the gospel in any city is as robust as the visibility of the church unity in that same city.

According to Visvasam and Emmanuel,

We want Movement Day to connect, catalyze, and foster collaboration against our enormous challenges in the city. We need to see much greater synergy between the church and corporate leaders.

Our vision is to see four thousand churches in Chennai sending one missionary per church to more than four hundred identified cities in India. If we are able to see this happen, it will be one of the greatest missionary achievements in the history of Christianity.[9]

WHAT THIS STORY TEACHES US:
Chennai Disrupted

Jesus will build His church.

It is breathtaking to see the vibrant presence of the church after two millennia in Chennai. Leaders have been faithfully working to build Jesus's church for a hundred generations. The size, breadth, and diversity of the church in Chennai gives one pause to celebrate what God is doing.

God is rearranging people groups across India.

With the internet technology boom and the industrial corridor growing in Chennai, it is important to pay attention to the growing opportunity to impact the professional class. The emergence of robust marketplace ministries is a great sign of hope in the city.

The movement of millennial leaders into cities like Chennai represents a new open door for the gospel to take root in the lives of many people.

Intelligent collaboration is necessary and urgent.

Given the enormous needs of the poor and the slum dwellers, now is an important time to align and aggregate the best thinking and resources to assist these vulnerable people. A greater Christian voice and influence in the place of governmental power is greatly needed on behalf of the poor and marginalized. A gathering like Movement Day provides the best research, as well as the opportunity to celebrate and inform collaboration between people who can help the city.

Chennai has an enormous opportunity to fulfill an apostolic calling to influence the rest of India's cities. This is an important vision to steward for India and the rest of the world.

A Prayer

Jesus,

We pray that You would be fully present among the poorest of the poor, the trafficked, and the slum dwellers. We also pray that You would reveal Yourself to the IT professionals and the automobile workers. Please bring Your people together to commission a missionary from every church across greater Chennai to reach many in the great cities of India.

Amen.

12

DUBAI

THE MANHATTAN OF THE MIDDLE EAST

But I have nothing definite to write to His Majesty about him. Therefore I have brought him before all of you, and especially before you, King Agrippa, so that as a result of this investigation I may have something to write.

—Acts 25:26

God *is rearranging people groups to populate the Middle East, that they may spiritually influence that vital region for the gospel.*

Jesus Followers in Dubai

I met Prem Nair and his wife, Sneha Rebecca, in August 2014. They were in the United States to attend the Global Leadership

Summit in Chicago and a family wedding in NYC. From 1984 to 1986, Sneha Rebecca's uncle pastored a church two blocks from where I lived in Jamaica, Queens. Small world.

Nair and some friends started a company called Red Orange a little over ten years ago. The company specializes in procuring and delivering goods and services to remote regions, including Afghanistan, Iraq, Kuwait, Lebanon, Sudan, Djibouti, and Kyrgyzstan. Red Orange has established itself as a trusted and reliable provider of sourcing and logistics services and is currently servicing more than three hundred open sourcing and supply contracts with the US military, NATO forces, other allied militaries, corporate groups, nongovernmental organizations, and relief agencies.

Headquartered in Dubai, Red Orange is supported by its globally networked procurement and supply chain teams. The company has moved huge consignments of supplies and equipment for its clients and has become known as a complete supply chain solution for challenging locations.

The Switzerland of the Middle East

According to the August 2014 *Forbes*, Dubai was listed as the seventh most influential global city in the world. It rises out of the desert as one of seven Arab Emirates. Its population of 2.5 million people makes it the largest city in the region.[1]

Dubai, considered the "Switzerland of the Middle East," is tucked in between Asia, Africa, and the Middle East, so half of the world's population lives within four hours by plane. It is a global commercial hub boasting the tallest buildings and largest malls in the world and beautifully architected mosques in every direction. It is a city of expatriates—nearly 90 percent of the residents come from other places to work in the city. Many expats are from Asia; India is the source of the largest group.

According to Nair, the economy is driven by diverse economies associated with tourism, trade, and financial services. Unlike much of the Middle East, Dubai does not depend as much on oil to drive its economy.[2]

However, Dubai is more than meets the eye. Nair offers three perspectives on the city:

> There is the traditional view of Dubai—what I call the "plastic" side of the city. It is a make-believe city, building endlessly. It is opulent, exaggerated, and exuberant. It is a playboy-type of city where people come with lots of money to play.
>
> There is a "second city" made up of 750,000 construction workers. Construction work is a modern form of Egyptian slavery, where 40 percent of the population comes to work at minimum wage in the desert sun and is never considered to be part of the culture. It is as if they don't really exist in the city. Construction workers practically live in boxes that are shipped back and forth by bus. Workers are hardly known by the city, except to be neatly boxed away. Many of these workers take loans to travel to Dubai looking for work. There is a lot of corruption in the construction industry in Dubai, and this population is trapped. It is very hard to get out of the cycle.
>
> The third audience in the city is the young, vibrant, and upwardly mobile young professionals. Young professionals represent the yuppie culture of Dubai. [They] enjoy the arts and finer things. There is a genuine appreciation [among young professionals] for those who are not as economically strong. [They have] a genuine desire to protect human rights among this demographic.[3]

The disparity between the glitter of a new city and the misery of the workers who built Dubai is stunning. It shimmers with its magnificent skylines and hundreds of thousands of laborers aching for a better life. Dubai is unique in that it has no income or corporate tax, providing an extraordinary environment for entrepreneurs to start companies.

The Gospel in Dubai

In September 2014, I met another remarkable entrepreneur from Dubai, Santosh Shetty, who leads a real estate company. We met in Singapore at a Generous Giving conference. Like Nair, Shetty is from South India and began to follow Jesus after having been raised in a Hindu family. He is passionate about impacting the Middle East and India with the gospel.

Shetty, Nair, and I share a common acquaintance, Ram Gidoomal, who lives in London and serves as the chairman of the Lausanne Movement. I will never forget a conference call between the four of us in March 2015. I was sitting in a Miami hotel room and we were all linked by teleconference. I was struck by the fact that three men from Hindu backgrounds were talking about the growth of the gospel in Dubai, India, and the globe.

Dubai is in great need of the gospel. It is estimated that thirty to fifty thousand people attend church out of a population of 2.5 million (roughly 1.5–2 percent). The leaders I met with are convinced that as the gospel flourishes in Dubai, it holds promise for the entire Middle East and the world.

One of the great accomplishments of the church in Dubai in recent years has been the successful creation of a 24–7 prayer expression across the city. Nair describes it this way: "For the past two years, sixty churches have adopted a day a month to pray over Dubai. . . . We have a common theme for every month. We also provide prayer training. This has resulted in growing unity among the churches. Doors are opening. There have been greater freedoms for the church."[4]

Churches praying together created the environment for the planting of the Global Leadership Summit. My observation is that the churches in Dubai are either Indian or international. It is difficult to bring together a globally diverse community, especially among a transient community. But I was quite impressed with the passion of the Global Leadership Summit's planning team to see the church united, leaders developed, and the city impacted.

Gospel principles are also spreading in the city beyond the church. For example, the average expat lives in Dubai for only three and a half years, and the stress of living this way has caused many marriages to crumble. Sona Kazanjian, a woman from Syria who has found extraordinary favor with the Dubai government, has initiated an effort to heal many of the broken marriages across the city by offering marriage retreats through a church network.

Kazanjian also has been the key link between the churches and the political community, helping open doors for churches to do more work together. When we spoke about leaders gathering in NYC for Movement Day 2016, Kazanjian said she wanted to invite leaders from Lebanon and the rest of the Middle East in order to be linked with the global body of Christ.[5]

Another expression of the gospel, called the Nehemiah Project, is emerging in the business community in Dubai. The group is hosted by Dubai Christian Business Associates and led by Saji Abraham.[6] Abraham is an Indian marketplace leader who works in the service industry. He has partnered with the Nehemiah Project to establish a community of business leaders who will network for the gospel and work toward strengthening fellow businesspeople through referrals and much-needed training to conduct business ethically. The Nehemiah Project motivates Christian marketplace leaders to think about biblical entrepreneurism and intends to establish numerous chapters in and around the Persian Gulf. Along with the Nehemiah Project, Dubai Christian Business Associates works closely with the giant South American Christian business team called ADHONEP Brazil, which has more than a thousand chapters.[7]

Nair says he wants to see this culminate in a strategic working group. "Based on the depth of our relationship strength, this strategy group would be able to address any initiative that we want to take on in Dubai."[8]

Dubai to the World

Given its identity as a hub for global commerce, Dubai is uniquely positioned to shape the future of global Christianity. Nair has been critically involved in identifying millennial leaders from his Dubai network who have been invited to shape the conversation for millennials globally. As discussed in chapter 7, millennial leaders are the bull's-eye for the current and future expression of gospel movements worldwide. Leaders under the age of twenty-eight are historically the initiators of most major spiritual movements.

I asked Shetty why, with all his professional and ministry demands, he is so committed to this particular vision. "I know what the gospel has meant to my family and to me," he says. "India has four hundred million people living in cities, as its urban population is growing very fast. I believe that cities are the new frontier of missions, and [I] want to make a difference with my life."[9]

The story of Dubai and the gospel is one of great irony. Leaders from wildly divergent church backgrounds have come to the city and created supernatural unity there. As leaders have met and merged their efforts, surprising happenings have furthered the growth of the gospel.

Within the past ten years the gospel expression has matured remarkably quickly throughout Dubai. In another ten years that expression will multiply many times over to impact this city, the Middle East, and the global church.

WHAT THIS STORY TEACHES US:

Dubai Disrupted

God is using kings and rulers for His own purposes.

The relative freedom of religious expression in Dubai is unusual in the Middle East, possible only because of the posture of the sheikh (the leadership that rules the Emirates) toward the church. Such freedom provides a remarkable opportunity to build multifaith alliances that lend credibility to the gospel.

God is raising up unlikely men and women to lead the gospel movement in Dubai.

I was encouraged to see men and women from Hindu backgrounds, varied Christian denominations, and the marketplace come together to impact Dubai and the Middle East. God is bringing people to Himself as a witness to diverse religious communities in an Islamic region.

A vibrant gospel movement is built on the foundation of concerted prayer.

The speed of the movement is proportional to the extent to which leaders are praying together. A two-year, 24–7 prayer effort has laid an important foundation for this movement. Prem Nair and his team have been elevated to take point for the effort. The neutrality of the marketplace leadership has brought credibility.

Dubai as a global city is uniquely connected to the world.

Dubai is a hub connecting Asia, Africa, and the Middle East. It is important that the global church pray for the progress of the gospel in Dubai and the city's ability to spread the gospel to some of the neediest places on earth.

God will use the marketplace leader as the vanguard of the movement.

The extraordinary pool of entrepreneurial gifting in Dubai will help plant marketplace expressions of the gospel throughout the Middle East. The next decade will be a thrilling season to witness what unfolds from Dubai, an oasis in the desert.

A Prayer

Jesus,

We worship You as the One who comes to us from the Middle East. You planted the gospel in Israel as a gift to the nations. May the gospel in Dubai be rooted deeply over the years ahead, and may it travel from this globally central city to half the world's population.

Meet the needs of the construction workers, the underclass, and the migrants. Influence and guide those with economic power. Unite Your internationally diverse church so that the authenticity of the gospel will be obvious to all.

So be it.

13

SINGAPORE

THE MANHATTAN OF ASIA

While Apollos was at Corinth, Paul took the road through
the interior and arrived at Ephesus.

—Acts 19:1

*C*ould there be a more strategic city in the world than Singapore?
It may be one of the best gateway cities for the gospel into all
of Asia, home to more than half of the world's population.

Asia's Manhattan

On July 5, 2015, I attended the Jubilee Day of Prayer at the
Singapore National Stadium. It was a magnificent gathering

of 51,000 Singaporeans, including Christians from diverse denominational backgrounds, as well as the president and prime minister, to commemorate the fiftieth anniversary of the nation. Singaporeans enjoyed a collective sense of celebration for all that had gone into achieving one of the highest standards of living in the world.

Singapore has been described as a swamp transformed into a city on a hill. Today it has earned one of the highest global rankings for clean governance and anticorruption.

At the celebration, I reflected on Christianity's beginnings in Singapore with leaders from Malay, Chinese, and Indian backgrounds. Their ancestors would have come to Christ out of Islamic, Buddhist, and Hindu traditions. Many first-generation believers planted the church in Singapore. And it required enormous courage to leave their childhood and family religions. The gospel was disruptive to the lives of those Christian pioneers.

The Singaporean church's legacy marries a deep sense of spirituality to a spirit of generosity. For instance, the Jubilee Day of Prayer raised more than $700,000 to benefit Singapore families.

In 2014, *Forbes* named Singapore the fourth most influential city in the world.[1] This is a remarkable achievement for a fifty-year-old island city-state. Considering that Asia has more than half the world's population with more than four billion people, this city of five million exercises extraordinary economic and spiritual leverage. Singapore is the Manhattan of Asia. It is no accident that God has raised up the church in Singapore amid a religiously diverse continent with billions of Muslims, Hindus, and Buddhists.

During my trip, I was hosted by Ezekiel Tan, general secretary for the Bible Society of Singapore (BSS), founded in 1823. Tan is a remarkable leader, giving direction to an incredible institution. The BSS is a sister institution to the American Bible Society and a member of the United Bible Societies. One of its founding leaders was William Wilberforce, a member of the British Parliament and an architect of the global abolition movement. The BSS, along with its counterparts in London, the United States, and Africa, provides Bibles for much of the world.

The Gospel in Singapore

The penetration of the gospel into Singaporean life is simply amazing. Ezekiel Tan says that it is estimated that 50 percent of the lawyers and 70 percent of the doctors in Singapore are Christian. Ezekiel estimated that Singapore has five to seven hundred churches, representing approximately one million Christians—or close to 20 percent of the population. The believing community is estimated to be two-thirds Protestant and one-third Catholic.[2]

The churches have a deeply collaborative spirit that predates Singaporean independence. In the 1930s, Chinese churches consolidated their working relationship into the Union of Chinese Speaking Churches in Singapore.[3]

For the next four decades, the unity of the church in Singapore would build slowly. A combination of grassroots efforts emerged to bring churches together alongside externally organized gatherings, including Here's Life Singapore, which involved 45 percent of the churches in the city.

In his book *In His Good Time*, Bobby E. K. Seng, author of many books on the spiritual history of Singapore, describes another defining moment in the spiritual history of Singapore at a Billy Graham crusade:

6 December 1978, National Stadium, 7:15 pm. The afternoon showers had only just stopped, leaving scattered puddles of water across the field. All around the Stadium, tiny streams of people with folded umbrellas under their arms, were making their way in through the entrances; the seats were half occupied. One big question loomed in the minds of all Christians: would the people of Singapore come or had they been too ambitious in booking the 65,000 seat Stadium?

Just four days earlier the island had been drenched with 512 mm of continuous rain, giving rise to one of the most massive floods in its history. Over 1000 people had to be evacuated.

Effective preparation for the Crusade only began in February 1978 with the formation of a 14-man Executive Committee. To put flesh and muscles to plans and policies, the Committee set up 20 Functional Committees. 237 of the 265 Protestant congregations committed themselves to the Crusade.

What happened on the first night of the Crusade is now a part of history. The Stadium was filled to capacity: 65,000 in attendance. Dr. Billy Graham's message on man's need to be "born again" was interpreted into Mandarin, Hokkien, Cantonese, Malay, and Tamil. 4,107 persons came forward on this first night.

For the five evenings, total attendance came to 337,000. 19,631 came forward to be counseled and of these 11,883 received Jesus Christ into their lives for the first time.[4]

That crusade was a turning point in Singapore's spiritual history. The growth of Christianity among the Chinese in Singapore has been breathtaking. Between 1930 and 1980, the Christian population grew nearly fourfold from 2.6 percent to 10.6 percent. The Chinese church continued to grow by another 30 percent up until 1990.[5]

Concurrent with the impact of the Billy Graham Crusade was the emergence of strong student movements in Singapore. Youth for Christ and Graduate Christian Fellowship began in the 1950s. Both of these movements, along with the charismatic movement of the 1970s, attracted thousands of young people. Additional youth movements were planted in the 1970s, including Inter-School Christian Fellowship, Navigators, Eagles Evangelism, Campus Crusade, and Fellowship of Evangelical Students. Student surveys indicated that a number of students were suspending their belief in the Chinese religions of their parents.[6]

The global trauma of World War II had become the womb for the birth of evangelical mission agencies. Thirty years after the war, these agencies were finding fertile soil on the islands of Singapore. The young people converted to Christianity in the 1970s became members of the professional class for Singapore for the next forty years.

The Unity of the Singaporean Church

Of the 261 Protestant churches in Singapore by the late seventies, 237 had participated in the Billy Graham Crusade. Within seventeen years, another 190 churches had been birthed, an increase of more than ten churches per year. By 1995, Singapore had 450 Protestant churches.

The National Council of Churches (NCC) has provided core leadership in expressing the unity of the churches in Singapore. The primary denominations involved in leadership for the NCC are the Methodists, Anglicans, and Lutherans. The NCC also has been officially recognized by the Singapore government.

Singapore serves the world as a great model of a denominationally diverse community that is committed to orthodox

Christianity while working closely with the local government. This positions the churches to be relevant at the societal and spiritual level.

The Bible Society of Singapore has played an important role in connecting the NCC and other movements that have emerged in the city. The Bible Society of Singapore has started a think tank (Ethos Institute for Public Christianity) in partnership with the NCC and Trinity Theological College to provide a place for leaders to thoughtfully consider how best to impact the city together.[7]

Love Singapore, "a unity movement motivated by love, fuelled by prayer, and inspired by a common vision,"[8] is one of the groups that has emerged in the city. Birthed in 1995 under the leadership of Lawrence Khong, senior pastor of Faith Community Baptist Church, Love Singapore aims to unify believers, serve the community, and adopt unreached people groups across the globe, among other things.[9]

In that same year, out of a Concert of Prayer gathering called A Day to Change Our World, a four-day Pastors' Prayer Summit was developed and has provided tremendous continuity for Singapore's faith community for two decades. This gathering has allowed hundreds of leaders across Singapore to gather annually to renew friendships, seek God together, and discover ways to collaborate. In recent years, the number of pastors who attend the event has ranged from three to five hundred annually.[10]

Singapore in 2015

Ezekiel Tan estimates that of the 700 churches in Singapore, 220 to 250 are affiliated with a denomination and 400 to 500 are independent. This speaks to the growth of new churches and, particularly, independent churches, and mirrors the trend of the approximately ten new churches started per year across Singapore. Ezekiel estimated that there are approximately 45,000 Methodists; 20,000 Anglicans; 28,000 Assemblies of God parishioners; 20,000 Presbyterians; 10,000 Baptists; 10,000 Church of the Brethren members; 8,000 Evangelical Free worshipers; 7,000 Church of Singapore churchgoers; 3,000 Lutherans; and 500 Salvation Army church attendees. Some megachurches have emerged with more than 20,000 attendees. Keeping such diverse congregations working in a common direction is extraordinarily challenging given the ethnic, denominational, and linguistic dynamics at play.[11]

So what is Tan's biggest concern for the Singapore church? The current plateau. "Young people are not as passionate about their faith as the previous generation. We have a Christianity without the cross."[12]

But that doesn't mean there isn't hope. Singapore is home to some remarkable leaders, including Edmund Chan, who birthed the Intentional Disciple Making Church movement. Chan has built an impressive global network with his philosophy of ministry: "Think Big, Start Small, and Build Deep. Nothing less than a global vision is worthy of a global God!"[13]

Chan has built significant relationships with global leaders like Randy Pope at Perimeter Church in Atlanta, Georgia:

> When [Randy and I] eventually met, I found a kindred spirit. Randy said with his characteristic tongue-in-cheek humor, "Are we twins?" Our hearts were immediately knitted together by the Lord, and Randy Pope expressed his strong support of the Global Alliance of Intentional Disciple Making Churches. After this,

other influential disciple-making senior pastors rallied behind this young movement.[14]

Chan has traveled the globe to speak to thousands of leaders about being intentional in their disciple making. He challenges them to not only grow big churches but also mentor leaders to be passionate, disciple-multiplying followers. "Paul didn't say, 'I am committed to Christ,' but, 'I am crucified with Christ.'"[15] This is a timely message for the church in Singapore and the rest of the world.

One of the greatest signs of hope I saw in Singapore was Hope Church International. The church began in 1991 with five people in a fellowship group. Today a global community of Hope Church fellowships thrives in thirty-five countries. I met with the senior pastor, Jeffrey Chong Hock Joo, along with two millennial staff members, Dennis and Timothy. I was impressed and encouraged to learn that the church has more than a thousand young people in attendance every week. The environment of the church provides younger leaders the freedom to create initiatives to reach young people from grade school to university.

I traveled with Jeffrey, Dennis, and Timothy to their church. They were hosting an international training conference for young leaders from Asia, Africa, and Europe. The leaders' hunger to learn was remarkable. I met with them and answered questions for close to an hour.

I also had lunch with Guna Raman, a church planter in Singapore working with Redeemer City to City. Raman is from an Indian background and is providing training for church planting. Given the extraordinary influence of Singapore and the enormity of Asia, a church-planting movement from the island city-state of Singapore has global implications. Hope Church is, in fact, a training movement for millennial leaders on all of the major continents.

God is at work in Singapore not only among the churches and their networks but also within the remarkable community of marketplace Christians—one of the most impressive marketplace communities in the world.

In 2014, I met Randy Teo, who was planting a chapter of Prime Movers. Prime Movers was started by Chip Ingram, who has a radio audience of a million people a week. The vision of Prime Movers is to help marketplace Christians discover their holy ambition. Given the enormous challenges in Asia, groups like Prime Movers need to be multiplied in every major city.

WHAT THIS STORY TEACHES US:

Singapore Disrupted

God is sovereignly at work.

Fifty years ago no one would have predicted that God would choreograph such a powerful advance of the gospel just as Singapore would emerge as a significant financial capital. God has honored the sacrifices of many pioneers in Singapore, including those of many first-generation Christians. Singapore is extraordinarily well positioned to continue to influence the spread of Christianity to other major Asian and global cities. The impact of the church in modern-day Singapore is the fruit of the historic vision of global church leaders like William Wilberforce.

Unity is rooted in prayer and manifested in evangelism.

The prayer movement of Singapore has been active for more than twenty years. God has used significant historical moments like the Billy Graham Crusade of 1978 and the Jubilee Day of Prayer in 2015 to stimulate unity and evangelism. The Pastors' Prayer Summit has provided an annual rhythm of leaders gathering to deepen relationships and seek God together.

Unity that is committed to the whole church and the whole city is an effective witness for the gospel.

The church in Singapore has been sensitive to the needs of those less fortunate. It has worked closely with the government to define the city's greatest needs. The denominational breadth of the unity movement is an enormous sign of hope for cities around the world.

Catalytic leaders are important to the ignition and sustained expression of unity in a city.

The gospel in Singapore is indebted to past and present leaders who have worked to keep the church united. The leaders interviewed in this chapter are a small sample of the enormous breadth of Christian leadership committed to the whole Singapore church.

It is equally important to keep an eye on the future, to empower current millennial leaders to reignite a gospel movement in Singapore. Every new generation needs identified and empowered leaders to lead into the next twenty years. This is Singapore's greatest immediate challenge and the challenge of every major city in the world.

A Prayer

Jesus,

We as the global church pray for Singapore. We are awed by all You have done in the past fifty years. We thank You for courageous men and women You have raised up to lead the church. May You raise up a new generation of millennial leaders who will multiply the influence and impact of Singapore around the world. We pray that Singapore will truly mature into an Antioch for the great cities across all of Asia.

We who serve You agree.

14

PORT-AU-PRINCE

LAZARUS ON OUR DOORSTEP

During this time some prophets came down from Jerusalem to Antioch. One of them, named Agabus, stood up and through the Spirit predicted that a severe famine would spread over the entire Roman world.

—Acts 11:27–28

How does the Western church respond to Lazarus at its doorstep? How the North American church responds to the crises in Haiti and Port-au-Prince is a barometer of its own spirituality.

—Don Golden, senior vice president, World Vision

Shaken Awake

The earthquake occurred at 2:53 p.m. local time on Tuesday, January 12, 2010.

I was sitting in the New York City Leadership Center conference room in Queens. Across the table from me were my colleagues Denis Baril and Tom Nolan, both of whom had spent significant time in Haiti. As news of the earthquake unfolded, these men were visibly shaken.

Ten weeks after the earthquake, I traveled with World Vision and a team of US church colleagues to see the damage and assess the interventions taking place. It was the closest thing I had seen to 9/11 in Manhattan. In fact, given the death toll, it felt like 9/11 times eighty.

Rubble was strewn in every direction. Hundreds of thousands of people whose homes had collapsed were living in makeshift tent cities. Those whose dwellings remained were afraid to go inside for fear of aftershocks and further collapse. People slept in the streets for months (nearly eighty thousand were still living in tent cities five years later).[1] We saw dozens of people who had lost limbs as a result of buildings falling on them during the quake. Fear spread as an epidemic of cholera broke out.

It was overwhelming to see the need and the outpouring of compassion. World Vision was feeding one million people each month. John Hasse, World Vision national director, describes the organization's interventions after the earthquake: "We provided water, tents, and initial shelter for 150,000 people. It was the most complex emergency disaster that we had ever responded to."[2]

Longer-term interventions included growing fruit trees to serve as an antidote to the almost complete deforestation of the country. Nearly all of the trees have been cut down to provide fuel, which has upset Haiti's climate cycles.

My own experience in Haiti was a microcosm of many Americans' experience. The nation is in our own backyard, yet I had very little working knowledge of it, even though America has an identified diaspora population of "156,000 Haitians in Metro NYC and, by one estimate, possibly up to 400,000, including illegal aliens."[3]

Don Golden offers this historical perspective, which is important for the Western church to consider when evaluating the need to engage in Haiti, and Port-au-Prince in particular:

> Haiti occupies a place of special concern for the US church. As American Christians respond with compassion and justice to the great causes of our day, Haiti stands out in both need and moral urgency as deserving special attention.
>
> Geopolitically, Haiti occupies a unique place. That's because, while all the indices are improving in the fight against extreme poverty (those without clean water and women dying in childbirth have been cut in half since 1990, and the cases of HIV/AIDS are down 25 percent), Haiti represents a special category of countries where poverty is becoming harder and harder to reach. Extreme poverty (those living on less than $1.25 per day) is increasingly more common in what the Office of Economic Cooperation and Development (OECD) calls "fragile states"—that is, countries that are unwilling or unable to care for their people. In states like Syria, South Sudan, Liberia, and the Democratic Republic of the Congo, conflict and poor governance make poverty intervention difficult or impossible. Global threats such as Ebola and violent jihadism are taking root. Of the fifty-one fragile states identified by the OECD, Haiti is the only one located in the Western hemisphere.
>
> Since it was founded in 1804 as a successful slave rebellion, Haiti has struggled for a legitimate and viable place in the

international community and the global economy. And since its birth, US policy has been a consistent force in shaping Haiti. From the occupation of Haiti by the US Marines during WWI to the US support of the Duvalier dictatorships, from the proliferation of offshore manufacturing to the Farm Bill, Haiti's fate has been inextricably linked to the interventions of its superpower neighbor. Despite these ties and notwithstanding the brief spike in interest and compassion following the 2010 earthquake, the American public is either unaware of or holds negative stereotypes about Haiti as a "black hole of need," a "basket case" country, or simply a nation beyond hope. . . .

Like Lazarus beckoning the rich man or Bartimaeus calling out to Jesus from the roadside, just seven hundred miles from the shores of the wealthiest and most powerful church in the history of the Christian mission, Haiti calls out for compassion and justice. Christians should recognize the voice of Christ in the suffering cry of the Haitian people as a rallying cry to a unified and historic response.[4]

The situation in Haiti has become even more urgent since the earthquake. The depth of suffering will continue unabated until people of goodwill step in on a significant scale to provide the basic necessities of life—clean water, access to education, economic opportunity, and adequate housing. Most important, future generations of Haitians and persons living globally in fragile states need to be self-sustainable.

Port-au-Prince

Almost forty million people reside in the Caribbean Islands, and about 10 percent live in or adjacent to Port-au-Prince. The modern-day Port-au-Prince metropolitan area has approximately

3.4 million people, and nearly 40 percent of Haiti's population lives there. The city is a place of extraordinary contrast between a few wealthier neighborhoods and areas of extreme poverty coupled with growing violence.

According to John Hasse, the quake exposed the challenges of the country. Millions of people are still living without housing. A large number of the buildings collapsed, and thousands of government workers were killed. Additionally,

> The city challenges your senses and the way you view life. It challenges the way you see life on earth—the way millions of people live. There is poverty on the street with everyone always asking for something. Children are begging. Women are limping along on one leg. They are trying to get enough money to pay for food for the next day. It is truly a survival culture. . . . The greatest needs of people living in the city are: security and good governance, given the propensity for corruption; consistent health and nutrition; clean water (40–50 percent of people in the country do not have access); the [church's challenge] to look at the life holistically, not just strictly spiritually; energy issues—fuel costs are difficult for Haitians.[5]

The Earthquake as a Wake-Up Call to the Haitian Diaspora

Mullery Jean-Pierre moved to Brooklyn from Haiti as a child in 1964. His father founded Beraca Baptist, a Haitian church in Brooklyn. Several years after his father died, Jean-Pierre became pastor of the church. He returned to Haiti for the first time in 2000, after a thirty-six-year absence.

> When I came back to Haiti for the first time in 2000, I saw that the country had deteriorated. The airport was still in terrible

condition. Everything seemed to have gotten worse. I came back heartbroken.

Many of the Haitian diaspora had vowed never to return to Haiti. Every Haitian had misery stories of Haiti as a homeland. The earthquake woke us up. Many second- and third-generation Haitians began going back to Haiti to consider what they could do.[6]

Jean-Pierre, who is ordained in the Converge denomination and gives oversight to Haiti for the denomination, was part of the World Vision March 2010 delegation to his homeland. He joined me again, along with a Grace Brethren group, in August 2010. During his travels he helped incubate a number of efforts across Haiti, including church planting, pastor training, and job development. He has been able to stimulate a number of child sponsorship efforts with both Converge and World Vision. His work with BILD International has helped train 1,700 leaders to grow healthier churches in Haiti.

Jean-Pierre has been effective not only on the ground in Haiti but also as a bridge builder between Haitian churches and US churches. I believe Jean-Pierre is the most respected Haitian pastor from among the three hundred Haitian churches in metro NYC. He has an unusual ability to work easily across the spectrum of racially and denominationally diverse leaders.

Today Jean-Pierre's greatest burden has to do with young people who are completely idle. Everyone is looking for a handout. The estimated average age of the island nation's current population is now fifteen to seventeen. Those adults who can, leave the island.

From the New York City Leadership Center, Sharon Cushing has been the hub for our contribution to a growing collaborative movement. Her enthusiasm for Haiti began several years ago when she joined with her friends Jeanette and Chris (a Haitian national) to assist several Christian schools in Haiti. These schools now serve hundreds of children, and two of the schools have become self-sustaining. Another school in an area southeast of Port-au-Prince is thriving with 120-plus students and a new school building under construction to house more.[7]

An Emerging Strategy: The 2015 Vision Trip

In April 2015, a dozen leaders representing a mix of NYC pastors and Haitian leaders traveled together to Haiti. The team was composed of five Haitian church leaders, a team of four from Christ Tabernacle, and our New York City Leadership Center team. Pastors Mike and Adam Durso from Christ Tabernacle helped Jean-Pierre plan and facilitate the trip. Mike had visited Haiti nearly forty times during his thirty years of ministry at Christ Tabernacle. Adam, his son, is one of the most effective voices in urban America encouraging emerging leaders to step into significant roles of leadership. Christ Tabernacle, with an international congregation, is one of the great church stories in NYC. Nearly one thousand people attend the church's prayer meetings every Wednesday night.

John Hasse and Dave Snyder of World Vision hosted our team. We had a remarkable five days together in the country. The objective of the trip? To explore what it would look like to create a decadal plan to impact a fragile state like Haiti.

We were able to see both the debilitating poverty of the countryside and the struggle for survival in the metropolis that is Port-au-Prince. We visited communities where people walk for miles to receive basic health care. Communities are susceptible to typhoid and other forms of misery due to unsanitary conditions, especially lack of clean water.

On the hopeful side, some leaders and communities were eager to work together. In the most impressive act of generosity we saw, a Catholic church donated property to World Vision. A state-of-the-art leadership center was built on the property to train leaders and host the community, providing an oasis for those navigating the harsh realities of their world.

The night before we returned to NYC, John Hasse hosted several leaders in his home. A diverse group ranging the evangelical–Catholic spectrum came together to consider how the faith community could make a measurable difference in Port-au-Prince and throughout the country. We were asking questions like, What would it take to see all Haitians have access to clean water? What would it look like to see new industries incubated that could provide work for young people for the next generation? What can be done to plant and grow more and better churches to meet Haiti's challenges, while collaborating intelligently with the North American church?

Out of our discussion emerged a decadal plan to impact Haiti. The foundations of the plan are:

1. *To call the global church to pray for Haiti and other fragile states.* Fifty-one fragile states represent 19 percent of the global population but 50 percent of global poverty. By 2030, that number will grow to 70 percent of global poverty.
2. *To develop a coalition of Haitian and North American churches that will commit to working together to create measurable progress over the next decade in Haiti, starting with Port-au-Prince.* It is critically important to aggregate leadership and best

practices around the greatest needs, which are far too great for any one agency or one network to address.

3. *To use Movement Day in New York City as an annual educational and mobilization platform to effectively engage leadership.* Movement Day will also be launched in Haiti to create a vehicle to more significantly unite the churches of the country to work together. Building the unity of the church across the nation and between Haiti and the United States is of paramount importance for the health of both church communities.

4. *To create annual vision trips.* The goal is to have leaders from North America come and see Haiti's needs firsthand, foster relationships with Haitian leaders, and experience the interventions that are being implemented.

This plan is intended to bring about measurable spiritual and economic progress for the country, impact hundreds of thousands of Haitians with quality-of-life improvements, strengthen Haitian churches, and guide the North American church in faithfully modeling and mobilizing in response to Jesus's justice-and-mercy mandate. Jesus's challenge in Matthew 25 is to care for the poor as a sign of our belonging to Him.

WHAT THIS STORY TEACHES US:
Haiti Disrupted

God can use tragedy to awaken His people.

Just as God awakened the US church to the needs of NYC after 9/11, the 2010 earthquake has awakened the Haitian diaspora and the US church to the gravity of injustice and need in Haiti.

We have been invited to share God's concern for the Haitian people and respond accordingly.

God can do immeasurably more by aggregating His people to work together.

We recognize our complete inability to make a significant difference in Haiti (or any fragile state) without a careful consolidation of goodwill, best practices, and resources. If we are able to foster intelligent collaboration, recognizing the unique contributions of each partner, we can make unimaginable progress over time.

Times are urgent.

Without the effective and urgent intervention of people of faith, Haiti will continue to languish, and its people will suffer. We must gather people of goodwill, who have the capacity to make a difference, to bring hope and a future to millions of vulnerable people.

The credibility of the gospel is at stake.

Haiti provides us an opportunity to prove the reality of Matthew 25 discipleship—a commitment to encounter Jesus among the poorest of the poor. Here we can demonstrate that the church can be organized and galvanized to bring about measurable progress in the most difficult places on earth. We are being given a chance to show the world the fulfillment of Jesus's promise: "I will build my church, and the gates of Hades will not overcome it" (Matt. 16:18).

A Prayer

Jesus,

We pray that You would awaken Your church to enter into the depth of Your concern for the Haitian people. Mobilize and enlighten Your church to know exactly how to respond to the centuries of unending agony experienced by millions of people.

May Your church make steps in the decade ahead that will demonstrate what Your people can do to elevate the lives of others in great suffering. Build a depth of unity between the Haitian church and the North American church that will result in hope for future generations.

Amen.

15

PRETORIA AND KIGALI

THE GOSPEL IN URBAN AFRICA

So [Philip] started out, and on his way he met an Ethiopian eunuch, an important official in charge of all the treasury of the Kandake (which means "queen of the Ethiopians"). This man had gone to Jerusalem to worship, and on his way home was sitting in his chariot reading the Book of Isaiah the prophet.

—Acts 8:27–28

Nowhere in the world do we see greater pain and greater possibility than in Africa. I have traveled to Africa almost every year since 1998 and have found no place else that restores one's soul quite like this vast, beautiful continent.

Pretoria, South Africa

The South African church—blacks and whites working together—played an important role in dismantling apartheid as an institution. The church prayed and worked behind the scenes to influence the De Klerk government to release Nelson Mandela from prison. The transition from pre-apartheid to post-apartheid was remarkably peaceful.

Mandela was released from prison in 1990, and four years later he was elected the first black African president of the country that had imprisoned him for twenty-seven years. It was breathtaking to see so much political progress in such a short time. Mandela's life embodied the centuries of struggle between races and classes in South Africa.

Pretoria is the administrative capital of South Africa, with a metropolitan population of nearly three million people. During my first trip to Africa in 1998 with Ray Bakke, I saw the contrast between the slums of Soweto (Southwest Township), next to Johannesburg, and the presidential palace in Pretoria. The Soweto community I visited was surrounded by barbed wire and had limited access to outdoor toilets. The poverty was grinding. Yet I shared with Soweto citizens the hope and joy of seeing the homes of Nelson Mandela and Desmond Tutu across the street from each other—probably the only street in the world with addresses for two Nobel Peace Prize winners.

A governing factor of city life in the country is crime, one of the most significant challenges facing urban South Africa in the post-apartheid era. Alan Platt, founder and senior pastor of Doxa Deo Church in Pretoria, ventured into this context of crime and violence in his city. In regard to the experience that transformed his perspective, he says, "I was invited by a local policeman in my congregation to travel with him on his night ride around the city. I was flabbergasted in seeing how people lived—the crime, the prostitution, and the hopelessness I saw in every corner of my city. I was determined to change our paradigm of church."[1]

I first met Platt in July 2013 in Bangalore, India, at the Lausanne conference. We've also crossed paths in the United States a few times and had the chance to discuss our respective work. Platt, a brilliant theologian and a powerful speaker, has publicly addressed the theme of citywide transformation on five continents.

Jurie Kriel, Platt's pastoral colleague and senior leader on one of the Pretoria campuses at Doxa Deo, says the culture of crime within the South African context is seen as normal. "Poverty and fatherlessness contribute to the culture of violence in our nation. We are facing extraordinary challenges politically and spiritually."[2]

The Birth of Doxa Deo

Against this backdrop of crime and poverty, Doxa Deo (Latin for "glory of God") was founded in 1996. In the past twenty years, it has grown to twenty campuses across South Africa and the world, including the United Kingdom, Germany, and New Zealand. Its weekly attendance is now thirty thousand. Its vision and strategy have become a global best practice for how a church can have an impact on a city.

During my April 2015 visit to Pretoria, Platt and the Doxa Deo team gave us a tour of the city and an overview of their work. The church and its network partners, called "fraternals," are working to address the more than 50 percent unemployment rate among young people. We saw one of Doxa Deo's major initiatives, People Upliftment Program (POPUP), a nonprofit that provides skills training for the unemployed. We also visited one of seven orphanages that have been established to focus on various needs of the children in the city, toured the high school on the Doxa Deo campus, and stopped at an integrated school with students from diverse backgrounds learning together (with exceptional academic results). The students at these schools represent the future of South Africa.

In addition to seeing the work of Doxa Deo and its partners in Pretoria, we participated in City Changers Movement Day, hosted by Doxa Deo leadership. It was thrilling to witness three hundred members of the body of Christ gathering from across the city to share stories of what God is doing throughout Pretoria. One of the great global stories emerging from South Africa has been the leadership of Graham Power in both the Global Day of Prayer and now the Unashamedly Ethical movement. He cast a vision at City Changers Movement Day for ways the global body of Christ can stimulate change in the marketplace. Doxa Deo demonstrated its ability to host a world-class event for the city.

Kigali, Rwanda

Kigali, a city of more than 1.1 million people, is the hub of every political, cultural, educational, and financial development for the country of Rwanda. I made my first trip there in 2003, just nine years after the hundred-day Rwandan genocide that claimed the lives of an estimated one million people. When you first land in Kigali, the terrain reminds you of Vermont. The picturesque and spectacular "land of a thousand hills" is also known as the "Alps of Africa."

After my first few days in Rwanda, I no longer saw Vermont but, rather, a giant cemetery. We visited the National Genocide

Memorial in Kigali where, on a fairly modest property, 250,000 people are buried. Meeting genocide survivors and observing their profound grief, and often tears, was heart-wrenching.

I concluded that the only passage in Scripture that can make sense of life and death for Rwandans may be Isaiah 53—the description of the suffering Servant—where they can finally identify with someone who knows by experience the kind of violence they have seen.

At the time the church and local government were wrestling with the question, How do you rebuild not only a city and a country but also a culture? I've been struck over the past decade by the world's efforts to help answer that question through the outpouring of compassion for Rwanda. The global community has partnered with the Rwandan community in remarkable ways. My primary exposure to this worldwide effort has been through the work of World Vision.

During my first trip to the country, I met Kofi Hagan, a twenty-five-year national director for World Vision in a variety of African contexts. World Vision has deployed Hagan into a series of gigantic crises. He saw the impact of the Ethiopian famine, which took a million lives from 1983 to 1985; the beginning of the AIDS crisis in Uganda in the 1980s; and the Rwandan genocide in 1994. I don't know of anyone else in the world who has witnessed all of these tragedies in person.

My team at Concerts of Prayer Greater New York, the New York City Leadership Center, and World Vision worked carefully together from 2003 to 2013 to engage the church of metro NYC in meeting the needs of Rwandan communities. I also traveled with pastoral teams into Kigali almost every year for a decade. While in Kigali, our racially diverse NYC team met with pastors and business leaders in the city, often at Hôtel des Mille

Collines, better known as Hotel Rwanda. We talked about a model for working together across racial lines. This was largely possible because of our two cities' interestingly similar racial journeys—from violence and traumatic injustice to powerful unity and collaboration across racial divides.

During that ten-year period, the NYC churches responded with great generosity—sponsoring more than five thousand children in Rwanda. Over a period of years, we could see the transformation in Kigali, as well as in the rural communities of Rwanda. Children who used to be barefoot now had shoes to wear, schools to attend, and homes that no longer leaked when it rained.

From 2003 to 2008, World Vision saw the number of sponsored children countrywide grow from a few hundred to nearly forty thousand. The sponsorship model effectively pools financial resources to create schools, arrange access to clean water, generate microfinance opportunities, build housing, and provide food security for communities.

Since 2005, Saddleback Community Church has sent 1,200 members to serve the churches of Rwanda through the PEACE Plan. Today more than four thousand Rwandan churches have partnered with the PEACE Plan and mobilized thousands of volunteers to serve and invest in their communities. The PEACE Plan, a church-to-church strategy that uniquely helps the whole person and the whole family for their whole lives, emphasizes:

- Planting churches that promote reconciliation
- Equipping servant leaders
- Assisting the poor
- Caring for the sick
- Educating the next generation[3]

President Paul Kagame—the military leader who stopped the genocide in 1994 with limited international support—has partnered effectively with global leaders to elevate Kigali and Rwanda to rank among the fastest-growing economies in Africa. Less than twenty years after a million-casualty genocide, Rwanda became a renewed nation experiencing fresh hope and prosperity.

Saddleback pastor Rick Warren has forged a remarkable partnership with Kagame. Together they have envisioned a future for Rwanda. In 2013, eight years after Saddleback's partnership with Rwanda began, Warren, along with a delegation of thirty-eight staff and volunteers, traveled to the African country. Warren addressed the nation on its second annual National Day of Thanksgiving. Thousands of Rwandans gathered at the National Amahoro Stadium, and thousands more tuned in online and on TV and radio as Warren challenged the nation to persevere as a model for the rest of the world. Warren made this visit, his first international appearance after his son's tragic death, because, in his own words, "Rwanda understands pain, suffering, and loss."[4]

Meeting President Kagame

In April 2013, I was part of a team of metro NYC leaders who traveled with Rich Stearns from World Vision to meet with President Kagame. The president tells a remarkable story of growing up in a Ugandan refugee camp. He was trained militarily in Uganda and eventually led the effort to stop the genocide in Rwanda. Kagame became president after the genocide and has served for three terms.

In our interview with him, one of us asked how he could lead after the country had been through such a traumatic season.

I was struck by his response, in which he said, "I have disciplined myself only to look forward. The past is past and cannot be changed."[5]

Kagame has had to lead his country through turbulent times. Significant internal conflict rages in neighboring countries like the Democratic Republic of the Congo and Burundi—conflict that can spill across the border at any time.

Kagame has instilled a sense of national pride in Rwanda and does not allow the usage of distinct tribal names, thus preventing infighting between tribes. Creating a sense of safety is a critical function of an effective leader.

Kagame also has instituted a monthly mandatory exercise for the residents of Rwanda to clean the streets, thereby promoting a national culture of cleanliness and discipline. He also has created an economic climate that is stimulating surprising growth in this landlocked country.

As one of the world's fastest-growing economies, Rwanda has demonstrated the powerful role of entrepreneurship in reconstruction and reconciliation. According to *Forbes*, "The country's annual GDP growth has averaged 8 percent over the past several years, and the percentage of people living in poverty has declined significantly. Within the next five years, Rwanda aims to become what it describes as a knowledge-based, service-oriented economy with middle-income country status."[6]

WHAT THESE STORIES TEACH US:
Africa Disrupted

Enormous populations are impacted by historic injustice, disease, and conflict.

As we take seriously the realities of disease, crime, and poverty, we need to engage God and the global church on behalf of Africa's cities. Also, the poverty and disadvantage of African populations should motivate us to assist global cities in great need.

The global community has much to celebrate with the African church. The African church is one of the fastest-growing churches in the world. Many people have emerged from great seasons of suffering with a tremendous faith. Many of the great leaders in the church, both now and historically, have come from Africa. The Cape Town Lausanne Congress of 2010 put on display the great spirituality and depth of the African leadership that is impacting the world.

Strong leadership is indispensable in the spiritual, political, and business realms. This chapter highlights the work of leaders like Alan Platt of Doxa Deo, Kofi Hagan and Rich Stearns of World Vision, Rick Warren of Saddleback, and Rwandan president Paul Kagame. Each of these men accepted and rose to enormously challenging leadership tasks. Each one saw with open eyes the dire circumstances, envisioned what could be, and courageously led others to successfully fulfill vision.

International and multiracial partnerships are powerful and necessary. As the world globalizes, it is both increasingly possible and imperative to acknowledge and study the great challenges of various societies and ways to address them. We can and must engage, learn, and collaborate in multiethnic teams of leaders. Global partnerships will model, better than ever before, the unity of Christ's body before the watching world.

A Prayer

Jesus,

We thank You for the African church and all that it has contributed—from the early African church fathers to two thousand years of Christian history.

We pray today for Your embrace—through the global church—of the orphan and the widow, the unemployed and the abandoned. We pray that You would use the church and its influence in government, economics, and education to create opportunities and hope for all of Africa.

We pray that the growing African church will spawn and mobilize missionaries across the continent and the world, especially into the stressed urban places.

Amen.

16

THE UNITED KINGDOM, THE GOSPEL, AND GATHER

And so we came to Rome.

—Acts 28:14

*T*he modern Christian movement has been profoundly shaped by Christian leadership from the United Kingdom. What would happen if a new generation of Christian leaders were raised up to impact the twenty-first century the way the United Kingdom church impacted the eighteenth and nineteenth centuries?

The World's Debt to the UK

In 1974, Billy Graham and John Stott birthed the vision of the Lausanne Congress to "take the whole gospel to the whole world by the whole church." These two men sounded the most significant challenge to stir and guide global Christendom in the past fifty years. Graham, the American evangelist, and Stott, the British pastor and theologian, gave voice to Jesus's call to unity and mission. They both significantly stimulated the expansion of the global church on all five continents.

After becoming a Christian in 1976, I was significantly influenced by three British theologians—John Stott, J. I. Packer, and C. S. Lewis. Their books—*Basic Christianity*, *Knowing God*, and *Mere Christianity*—were extraordinary influences on me. Their work shaped Christianity around the world. These men were, in turn, all shaped by the United Kingdom and its twentieth-century leadership role. They were the heirs of the great missionary and social movements birthed from their nation.

British preachers like Spurgeon and parliamentarians like Wilberforce invigorated the spiritual and moral contours of the globe, while Hudson Taylor and William Carey were heroes of the global missions movement.

In 2000, Winston Churchill was named the most important British citizen in history. He was also named the most important wartime leader of the twentieth century. I have read five of his biographies. Churchill's example is unsurpassed in regard to his leadership, courage, perseverance, and inventiveness. He stood alone in 1940 as Nazism engulfed all of Western Europe. The United Kingdom was within one lost battle of losing its freedom.

More recently, London's increasing influence has been recognized by *Forbes*, which in 2014 named it the most influential city in the world.[1]

The Changing Face of the Gospel in the United Kingdom

I have been exposed to the shifting influence of the gospel in the United Kingdom over the past couple years and can say that there are some amazing things happening in the country. Pastor Roger Sutton is the Gather national coordinator for the Evangelical Alliance in the United Kingdom, a group representing the country's approximately two million evangelical Christians. I met Roger in 2013 when he joined the Global City Leadership Community (GCLC). At our monthly GCLC meetings, he would give thrilling reports about God's work across the United Kingdom. He's been surprised by some of what the Evangelical Alliance has discovered:

> Our team was stunned to find 116 unity movements across the United Kingdom that we didn't know existed. We found these movements all across the UK in nearly every major city and town. These unity movements were birthed for mission and transformation.[2]

According to Sutton, about 10 percent of people attend church across the United Kingdom. All of Europe has been impacted by growing secularization. One of the great surprises to me has been that the majority of people attending church in London are either African or Caribbean. Christians are immigrating into the United Kingdom from the global South in enormous numbers.

In addition to growing secularization in the United Kingdom, "the number of Muslim converts in Britain has passed 100,000, fuelled by a surge in young white women adopting the Islamic faith. The figure has almost doubled in ten years—with the average convert now a 27-year-old white woman fed up with British consumerism and immorality."[3]

These are volatile times in the United Kingdom, given the global refugee crisis. Is it possible that God is uniting the church at historic levels to seize this new opportunity to be the welcoming arms of Christ to its newest citizens?

Gather: A Growing Movement

Sutton hosted our first in-person GCLC meeting in May 2014 in London. While we were all there, he also decided to convene a national gathering of unity movement leaders under the umbrella name "Gather."[4] More than one hundred leaders, on very short notice, made the effort to attend the event at the London Institute for Contemporary Christianity, founded by John Stott. The Gather meeting involved diverse leaders from many spheres—church, marketplace, arts, and politics—who shared a fervency to see the gospel more deeply penetrate their cities.

According to Sutton, "We began to discover these gospel movements in all of these cities—[movements] which were as old as eighteen years. We saw a need for an entity like Gather, which could become a 'network of networks.' We are [denominationally] neutral and not trying to advance our agenda beyond deepening friendship and advancing the work of each city."[5]

Sutton outlines the vision, strategy, and values of Gather like this:

The Gather vision is to see unity for transformation movements in every village, town, city, and borough. A good Gather-type movement is based on strong relational friendships, sustained prayer over a long period of time, and joint missional activity with a vision to see spiritual, cultural, and social transformation over a long period of time. They include not only church leaders but also leaders of Christian organizations and leaders in the cultural spheres.[6]

What does it take to have a healthy and successful movement?

- **Everyone involved.** This includes the majority of church leaders, Christian organizational leaders, and key Christian leaders in the cultural spheres.
- **Friendship and prayer.** A healthy and successful movement must be founded on strong relational friendships and sustained prayer.
- **Mission.** The group must share a regular joint mission with a special focus on service to the most vulnerable.
- **Transformational vision.** People must have a vision to see their place significantly transformed culturally, socially, and spiritually over the next thirty years.
- **Unity values.** The movement must be built on values of God's kingdom, not empire; honor, not criticism; inclusiveness, not exclusiveness; partnership, not competition.
- **Partnership approach.** This means linking (as one church in that city) significantly with the public, private, and third-sector partners to achieve lasting transformation.
- **Spheres focus.** Church leaders should release, train, and enable church members to be whole-life disciples with a transformational vision for their neighborhood and

workplace. They should form prayerful and relational networks within the spheres to see over time significant numbers of Christian public leaders in all the spheres at all levels.[7]

Sutton says God is working powerfully throughout the United Kingdom.

In Croydon (London), the churches have been praying and working together for many years. This has resulted in some exciting joint working with the civic authorities. There are more than 240 churches in the Croydon Church Forum. The Forum exists to help [churches] know what [other churches are] doing, work together on common mission, and pray together.

This includes the Croydon churches' Floating Shelter, which sees seventy churches work together to provide a bed and hot meal for homeless people for five months of the year. Other projects run by the Croydon churches include Christians Against Poverty, debt advice centers, food banks, club angels . . . school pastors, and chaplaincies in the council, college, shopping center, and Crystal Palace Soccer Club.

In Reading, a town outside London, the vast majority of church leaders meet together to pray every Wednesday morning and have done this for eighteen years. The churches of Reading are providing the civic authorities with over fifty families who are available to foster and adopt children.

In the north of England, in York, over 75 percent of the churches actively work together and have had joint mission and evangelism activities for over seventeen years. In London, twenty-eight of the thirty-two boroughs have their own expressions of the unity movement. These are just snapshots of the 116 movements across the United Kingdom which are reshaping how mission is being delivered across the country.

In Manchester, where I live, we have partnered in youth outreach with an initiative called the Message. This has provided coordinated activity around youth work. Between 2000 and 2002, there was a massive evangelistic outreach with Luis Palau. It helped our organization understand that effective outreach had to be preceded by practical service to the community.[8]

Sutton also told me about an effort in York called street pastors. According to the ministry's website, "Street pastors are trained volunteers from local churches who care about their community. They patrol in teams of men and women, usually from 10 p.m. to 4 a.m. on a Friday and Saturday night, to care for, listen to and help people who are out on the streets."[9]

During my March 2015 trip to the United Kingdom, Steve Clifford, the general director of Evangelical Alliance, hosted me in his home. He and his wife, Ann, are a winsome couple, and their affection for the church and for London is contagious.

Ann talked about her work as a street pastor. The previous night she had ministered on the street between 10:00 p.m. and 4:00 a.m. She described how she and her team prayerfully engage men and women as they emerge from the bars and clubs—often inebriated. This is a way for the church to establish a presence in the street, available to those who need to experience the grace of God.

Gather, Movement Day, and the Future

Sutton hosted me for a series of meetings in London in March 2015. For three days Sutton and I met with a number of London unity leaders, including those from All Souls Church and Hampton Trinity Brompton (HTB). HTB is the mother church for the global Alpha movement—a friendship evangelism model being used to impact millions of people with the gospel. We were exploring the possibility of having a Movement Day in London for the United Kingdom.

I was also privileged to stay with Ram Gidoomal, the Lausanne board chair and a board member of the New York City Leadership Center. He was born into a Hindu family before the 1947 partition of India. His family migrated to Kenya and then to London. As a university student, he became a follower of Jesus—one of the first members of his Sindi tribe to do so. He has since led fifty of his family members to faith in Jesus.

Also, Gidoomal, a successful businessman and leader, is highly respected in London and twice ran for mayor. His attendance at the London meeting made a strong impression on leaders we met with and lent credibility to our message.

Gidoomal speaks with real conviction on the value of Movement Day:

> Movement Day is able to bring together diverse parts of the church like nothing I have seen before. We have marketplace leaders, church leaders, and agency leaders all in the same room with the same passion for their city. What I have seen in New York City leads me to believe that every major city of the world would benefit from such an expression of unity and mission.[10]

Sutton sees a Movement Day in London in 2017 as the natural progression of Gather's efforts across the United Kingdom. He envisions leaders meeting in the next few years for:

1. **GatherSouth.** Building on the success of GatherNorth, which was held in Watford in autumn 2015, a one-day

conference will take place for Gather unit movements across the south and southeast of England.

2. **GatherSouthWest.** To be held in the Bristol area in 2016 for the southwest region.

3. **Workshops.** A series of workshops and training days will be offered to unity movements, covering areas such as how to start a unity-for-transformation movement, how to make whole-life disciples in the cultural spheres, how to engage with your civic authorities, and how to pray for your city.

4. **National sphere network days.** Gather will host a series of network days to bring together businesspeople, artists, medics, teachers, Christians in governments, and media specialists.

5. **Movement Day UK: London 2017.** Building on the success of Movement Day in New York, a two-day event in London will take place at Westminster Central Hall in early October 2017. This will provide a flagship event to heighten the awareness of the missional perspective of transforming our cities. Gather will work with a number of partners, making it the main ending event to the year of unity.[11]

Sutton believes the possible outcomes of hosting a regular Movement Day event in London over the next five years include the following:

- Significantly raising the missional perspective of unity for transformation in the nation
- Accelerating the vision for existing movements
- Kick-starting London unity

- Accelerating the vision for evangelism, millennials ministry, racial unity, and sphere networks
- Creating a comprehensive conversation with diverse expressions of the church regarding unity and mission together

Movement Day United Kingdom is a globally significant idea, given the enormous parts London and the United Kingdom play on the global stage. With Christians from the global south moving into London, God is rapidly rearranging the chess pieces of the global church. I believe He is doing this to address the newest challenges of migration, immigration, poverty, secularism, and urban youth.

WHAT THIS STORY TEACHES US:
The United Kingdom Disrupted

London and the United Kingdom have provided great historical foundations for the gospel and are continuing to be places of global influence.

It is important to remember our past and who God has used to shape us. The global church is forever indebted to the great missionaries, Christian politicians, and theologians from the United Kingdom.

God is birthing new expressions of missional unity like Gather to achieve larger purposes.

Given the enormous contemporary challenges facing the United Kingdom and all of Europe, the church has been confronted by a sense of both urgency and opportunity. The Evangelical Alliance is a historic expression of the global church. It is significant that Gather has its roots in a historic movement. That Sutton and his team are being given the freedom to create an entrepreneurial effort speaks to the depth of trust between leaders on the same journey.

Being aware of what God is up to is wise.

The Gather movement grew out of a fresh realization of all that God was doing throughout the United Kingdom. Having eyes to see and ears to hear is critically important as He creates new wineskins to influence greater numbers of people.

Sharing best practices globally is important.

Sutton has demonstrated a desire to learn and teach what God is doing nationally and internationally. He has brought several of his colleagues to participate in global conversations in places like Pretoria and NYC.

The foundations remain the same.

The work of city transformation is rooted in long-term, united prayer; trusting friendship; and seriousness about meeting the needs of people in the community. This is true around the world.

A Prayer

Jesus,

The global church is indebted to You for the great work You have done through men and women of past centuries in the United Kingdom. We are thankful for the work You've done to impact cities across the United Kingdom. Gather Your people

195

to love one another and celebrate what You are doing. Please provide the courage required to meet the greatest needs of our generation.

Amen.

17

GOTHENBURG AND BERLIN

THE GOSPEL IN URBAN EUROPE

Now those who had been scattered by the persecution
that broke out when Stephen was killed traveled as far as
Phoenicia, Cyprus and Antioch, spreading the word only
among Jews.

—Acts 11:19

As the Middle Eastern refugee crisis engulfs Europe, God is choreo-
graphing the nations of the world into cities where His church is
vibrant. He is turning the world upside down for His grander purposes.

The Gospel in Gothenburg

In September 2014, I made my first trip to Gothenburg, Sweden. I had become friends with notable leaders Daniel Grahn and Tomas Brunegård through the Global Leadership Summit and Halftime, an organization designed to help middle-age Christians evaluate what God may have in store for them during the last thirty to forty years of their lives, both of which Grahn had been the catalyst for bringing to Sweden. Grahn is a highly respected marketplace leader and networker among the body of Christ in Sweden. Brunegård is the president of the World Association of Newspapers and News Publishers.

During my visit, Brunegård gave me a tour of Gothenburg, showing me the spectacular waterways that connect the city to the world. With nearly one million people, Gothenburg is the second-largest city in Sweden, after Stockholm. Gothenburg has many universities and hosts some of the finest festivals in Europe. Its beauty attracts people from all over the earth.

Because of its neutral stance militarily in World War II, Sweden has been an attractive place for refugees. Approximately 15 percent of Sweden's population is immigrants. Two-thirds of the immigrants are from outside the European Union. For example, because of the upheaval in the Middle East, many displaced people from those areas have migrated to Sweden.

In 2015, half of the Syrian population of twenty million was displaced because of civil war in the country. CNN describes the conflict as "hellish." One in every five displaced people on the planet in 2015 was Syrian. Half of the displaced people were relocated inside of Syria. The rest were trying to get to Europe and places like Sweden.[1] A majority of these refugees are Muslim. Numbers show that the gospel has apparently

198

been reaching the Muslim population, as more Muslims have begun to follow Jesus in the past 15 years than in the past 1,500 years combined.[2]

Despite secularization's significant influence in Sweden, the country is seeing momentum toward a gospel movement. Grahn, Brunegård, and their network of friends have been working to promote citywide and nationwide Christian unity and collaboration.

Brunegård has been described as perhaps the most influential Christian marketplace leader in Western Europe, given his influential role as president of the World Association of Newspapers and News Publishers and former chairman of the board and CEO of Sweden's Stampen Group, a fast-growing media group and one of Sweden's largest newspaper owners. He represents the Christian marketplace engagement that is needed so badly to bolster the culture of cities.

In 2015, the Global Leadership Summit was held in cities throughout Sweden, including Stockholm, Gothenburg, Falun, Orebro, Linkoping, Malmo, and Umea. Thousands of Swedish church leaders are creating a culture in which the church can make a deep spiritual impact. The efforts in Gothenburg have been broad-based denominationally, guided by the diverse Swedish church teams that have traveled to Chicago for the summit and to NYC for Movement Day.

I participated in a leadership gathering at Smyrna Church, the largest Pentecostal church in Gothenburg. (In the past three years the church has baptized 450 Iranians. It also has provided a safe place for refugees to be cared for and to learn about Jesus through friendship evangelism and service.) Leaders came to the gathering from across Scandinavia to explore what it could look like to invigorate the gospel in more Scandinavian cities.

The meeting was encouraging because it showed the breadth of the Swedish church's hunger to impact cities.

The Gospel in Berlin

According to Brunegård, "Berlin is emerging as the new European capital."[3] At one time Berlin was the third-largest city in the world. German scholarship has been influential in academic circles, and many of the great scientists and theologians have German roots. According to Axel Nehlsen, executive director of Together for Berlin, the city is home to approximately 3.5 million people. It became the capital of Germany after the re-unification of East and West Germany. It is a city of foreigners, with five hundred thousand people from 190 different nations. It is also a city of students, with five major universities and 130,000 students.

Berlin, however, faces several challenges. It is still culturally and psychologically divided between East and West. The East operates as a "red" or communistically oriented city. People are paid unequal salaries between East and West, with higher salaries in the West. The city also has an 11 percent unemployment rate.

Immigrants continue to pose challenges to Berlin as well, and the situation has been only exacerbated by the Syrian refugee crisis. Despite the enormous challenges caused by absorbing so many refugees, Germany has emerged as the leading European voice in the crisis.[4]

The Religious Landscape of Berlin

According to Nehlsen, only 33 percent of the Berlin population belongs nominally to any Christian church. The majority of

Protestants are Lutheran and Reformed. About 10 percent of the population is Roman Catholic. The evangelical, Orthodox, and immigrant churches comprise 1.5 percent of the population each.

The largest group is the nonreligious at 60 percent. Nehlsen estimates that there are seven hundred churches with forty thousand people who would claim to be "born again." Berlin is home to six synagogues and twelve thousand Jewish people.

One of the fastest-growing religions is Islam, with 250,000 Muslims (2015 figure) and 130 mosques in Berlin. Six thousand Buddhists also reside in the city.

However, Christianity also has a presence. For example, the Evangelical Alliance is working in fifteen local communities, each of which holds its own annual prayer week and evangelistic campaign. And Together for Berlin (TFB) is an international initiative founded in 2002 to connect and encourage individuals, initiatives, communities, and churches to serve the city together. TFB is based on the Lausanne Covenant, calling "the whole church to take the whole gospel to the whole world."[5]

Nehlsen describes the transformation of Berlin after World War II:

> Between the years 1945 and 1950, the Allied troops had reign. In the 1950s and 1960s, Berlin experienced an economic miracle. Industry was developed because of the Marshall Plan. Berlin found itself in the middle of the global struggle between communism and democracy. In West Berlin, the church did well due to disillusionment with Nazism.
>
> In 1968, we had a revolution among the young people. They opposed their parents and focused on the guilt of Nazism . . . [particularly concerning] the Holocaust toward the Jews.
>
> The Berlin Wall finally came down in 1989, and we saw the Lord acting visibly in history—a reunited Germany in peace with

neighboring countries. That peace has remained for more than twenty-five years. We celebrated the twenty-fifth anniversary of the wall being torn down in October 2014.

There remain large differences between East and West. The election outcomes are different. In East Berlin 30–40 percent of the population is sympathetic with the communist party, compared to 5 percent in West Berlin. Berlin has become a new city with a lot of tearing down the old Berlin, a lot of building the new Berlin, and a lot of debt. Berlin is a lot like Boston—a very creative startup city. We have the largest number of startup companies across Europe.[6]

Nehlsen describes the 2002 beginning of TFB as creating John 17 efforts for unity. Jesus's John 17 prayer "that they may be one" motivated Berliners to explore different prayer initiatives, including prayer walks and praying in many small groups throughout the city. This was phase 1 for TFB.

The TFB leadership recognized that the larger denominations were stagnating and that Berlin had a history of being a "divided city." Fostering unity across the city was crucial and strategic. In the absence of any formal citywide coordination of activities, a "network of networks" was needed. TFB—with a desire to serve the vulnerable populations of Berlin, including prostitutes, addicts, and disenfranchised youth—stepped in to fill this vacuum.

Phase 2 focused on reaching all areas of the city with the gospel from a holistic kingdom perspective. TFB identified and connected initiatives around the city that were affecting local communities.

TFB efforts throughout the year are focused on the neighborhood level. They also hold biennial conferences for leaders and networks. In the odd year between conferences, the group hosts citywide festivals that bring the body of Christ visibly together in worship.

Phase 3 is to focus on personal relationships—identifying service and personal evangelistic efforts that are already showing great potential and strengthening them as catalysts for innovative citywide outreach.

Nehlsen describes the vision and mission of TFB as "an interdenominational network in the Greater Berlin area that connects and encourages individuals, initiatives, communities, and churches to serve the city. Our goal is to experience the positive effects of the gospel for as many areas of society as possible—through the prayer, witness, and practical service of Christians."

After thirteen years with the organization, Nehlsen has made some important observations:

> We aren't fans of Superman, who can do things perfectly. We are fans of Spider-Man, who is well networked. We want to do less ourselves and encourage others. Our role is to influence the thinking and attitudes of the spiritual movement across Berlin.
>
> The city is a complex living system. We have found over one hundred grassroots movements. We try to identify and start with innovators. We are part of a greater network, and we celebrate that reality. TFB is not an umbrella organization for a Christian city movement but an association that provides support for such movements. Wherever we can help Christians seek to reach the very best for Berlin, we gladly do it.[7]

TFB provides the following forums across Berlin:

- Prayer
- Intercultural relations
- Micah Challenge (social justice) and refugees
- Prison ministry
- Community organizing

- Youth Forum Berlin United
- Transform conferences

These forums provide vehicles for diverse Christian communities to network in the broad ecosystem of initiatives across the city. The resulting greater depth of relationships between members of the citywide Christian community produces greater transformational impact. The unity of the church breathes the aroma of belief across a city.

Leading Europe's Cities

In September 2015, Nehlsen's team hosted the All-European City Congress—a gathering of leaders from twenty-one European cities to discuss what God is doing in their cities. Against the backdrop of the Syrian refugee crisis, leaders are asking what the church can do together to make a way for the gospel to penetrate refugee cultures. Many of the networks of churches and Christian leaders in European cities are quite young. Yet they display a fresh hunger to encourage one another along in the critically important work of united prayer, collaborative evangelism, and service to our cities.

The European leaders are trusting God for a new spirit of renewal across the continent. God is radically rearranging the people of the world and bringing them into the great cities of Europe.

WHAT THESE STORIES TEACH US:
Europe Disrupted

God is moving unexpectedly in European cities.

Who would have imagined a few years ago that God would be bringing Muslims to the Christian faith in unprecedented numbers in new places like Gothenburg? God has raised up new and innovative work, out of Berlin's World War II ashes, as a model for the rest of Europe and the world.

God has strategically positioned marketplace leaders in Europe to impact the continent.

God is using leaders like Brunegård and Grahn to mobilize the Swedish church to engage the secular culture of Europe. The Global Leadership Summit has become an important rallying point for the body of Christ in Swedish cities.

God's Spirit is stirring cities across Europe.

The September 2015 gathering in Berlin is evidence that European leaders hunger to come together from all areas of the complex continent. Hundreds of cities are experiencing early stage unity and missional expression in new places.

A Prayer

Jesus,

Just as You called Paul to come to Philippi and plant the first European church, we pray that You awaken Your global church to the fresh opportunities in Europe. Thank You for sovereignly bringing the people of the world into the cosmopolitan cities of Europe.

We pray that northern, central, eastern, and southern Europe would be effectively linked. This one continent spans centuries of diverse church traditions. May You fully awaken Your church in all of its diverse expression. We pray for leaders who suffer from limited religious freedom. We pray for the tens of millions of people who have lost everything and have come as refugees to the great European cities.

Amen.

18

A GLOBAL SNAPSHOT
OF CITIES

You will be my witnesses in Jerusalem, and in all Judea and
Samaria, and to the ends of the earth.

—Acts 1:8

W hen God looks at planet Earth, what does He see?

He sees more than seven billion people. He numbers every
hair on every head. He knows everyone by name, and He numbers
everyone's days.

He invites all of us to share in His concern for the world—and for
its great cities.

Small World, Huge Task

Where does everyone live? According to *Operation World*, we can divide the globe into these regions by population:

Asia—60 percent of the globe in fifty nations

Africa—15 percent of the globe in fifty-six nations

Europe—10 percent of the globe in forty-six nations

Latin America (including Mexico)—8 percent of the globe in twenty-two nations

North America (US, Canada, Territories)—6 percent of the globe in five nations

Pacific Nations—1 percent of the globe in twenty-seven nations[1]

From 2010 to 2030, the global population is expected to rise from 6.9 billion to 8.3 billion—20 percent growth in twenty years. What characterizes this global population? The majority of this population resides in cities, is under the age of twenty-five, and lives on less than two dollars per day. The majority of people in human existence are urban, young, and desperately poor.

In June 2015, I was privileged to meet in Philadelphia with the regional directors (RD) of the Lausanne Movement. During that summer I conducted follow-up interviews to get regional snapshots of what was happening in the major cities around the globe. I asked each international deputy director three questions: (1) What are the major cities of your region? (2) What are your greatest challenges? and (3) What do you see as the greatest signs of hope?

Asia

East Asia

China and India alone represent nearly one-third of the global population, as they now exceed one billion people each. The geographic, linguistic, and religious diversity of Asia is extraordinary, representing fifty nations. The largest Buddhist, Hindu, and Muslim nations are all in Asia. Jesus Himself was an Asian-born baby who became an African refugee.

In China, which comprises the bulk of East Asia, the most well-known cities are Beijing and Shanghai. Other megacities include Guangzhou, Shenzhen, Chongqing, and Tianjin, which are all considered among the top sixty-six most influential cities according to the 2012 A T Kearney report.[2] According to David Ro, Lausanne RD for East Asia, several Chinese cities are merging into a conglomerate supercity. A plan is in place for Beijing to become a megalopolis of 130 million by the year 2030, by which time China is expected to be 30 percent urban. (Ro also points out that Hong Kong and Seoul are other important East Asian cities, and that, according to A.T. Kearney, Tokyo is a top-five city in terms of global impact.)

The good news is that modern-day China may be home to the fastest-growing church in history, with an extraordinary tens of thousands of conversions daily. Other signs of hope in East Asia include the Mission China Movement, whose vision is to mobilize twenty thousand Chinese missionaries primarily to travel to the West. In September 2015, one thousand pastors attended a Mission China Movement conference. Indigenous Chinese missions movements are on the rise, and missionaries are heading out into the world.

South Korea has sent ten thousand missionaries across the globe in each of the last two decades, and the number of known Korean missionaries is twenty-six thousand and still growing. But the South Korean missions movement is forecast to decline, given the trajectory of young adult engagement. The church of Seoul has lost much of its credibility; only 3 percent of young Korean people are staying in the church after they become adults. Meanwhile, China is expected to mobilize twenty thousand missionaries in the next decade or two. These missionaries will emerge from the cities and be effective tentmakers in places like Dubai.[3]

Southeast Asia

The largest cities in Southeast Asia include Jakarta, Bangkok, Manila, Ho Chi Minh City, Hanoi, Singapore, Kuala Lumpur, and Yangon. This complex region's cities represent Buddhist, Muslim, Hindu, Catholic, and communist contexts. Indonesia has the largest Muslim population in the world, but according to Philip Chang, RD for the region, Christianity in Jakarta has grown and is estimated to be 15–20 percent of the population. As of early 2016, the mayor of Jakarta is a Christian.

The greatest challenges in the region, according to Chang, include the rising disparity between the powerful rich and the powerless poor. As masses of people, including economic migrants and asylum seekers, search for employment in the cities, human trafficking becomes a huge issue. To engage the enormous and complex needs of major city populations, Chang points out the great need for much more effective discipling and equipping of lay leaders to integrate faith and work.

Signs of hope include the churches' understanding of their responsibility to engage their cities. Also, Christianity in the marketplace is beginning to thrive. Marketplace ministries, taking many expressions, are also emerging.[4]

South Asia

India dominates the South Asian landscape, surrounded by Pakistan, Bangladesh, Sri Lanka, and Nepal. The six primary metro areas are Mumbai, New Delhi, Chennai, Kolkata, Hyderabad, and Bangalore, all in India and all benefiting from major development. The Indian government foresees twenty cities with populations over one million people.

The macrostrategy of the Indian government is to develop one hundred "Smart Cities" with environments designed for economic growth and with the ability to absorb the massive population movement toward urban areas. As with China, India is expected to become 30 percent urban by 2030.

Finny Philip, the RD for South Asia, summarizes the greatest challenges facing Indian cities:

> Apart from the normal challenges of secularism, we see a rise of religious nationalism and materialism, triggered by globalization, growing very strongly in all Indian urban areas. Spatial and socioeconomic inequalities are evident in the urban sprawl, overcrowding, unemployment, crime, and environmental challenges. Migration patterns are a huge issue. For example, 250,000 migrants make the Delhi region their home every year. With the collaboration of Hinutva nationalism and corporate powers, our urban centers have become laboratories for "majoritarian vendetta." This collaboration has made our cities simmering reservoirs of hatred and violence. In the emerging cities there are constant conflicts between ethnic groups migrating from rural communities and the local population.[5]

Signs of hope for the Indian church include a greater receptivity toward the gospel. Enormous and broad collaborative efforts are emerging in the arena of united prayer and church planting. One effort under way has the support of evangelical, Pentecostal, and Catholic churches.

Christianity in the surrounding countries of Pakistan, Nepal, Sri Lanka, and Bangladesh tells a story of the extraordinary courage of leaders. For example, God has used leaders like Ajith Fernando to grow the church in Sri Lanka. James Dean of Karachi, Pakistan, has led the Pakistani church's partnership with the Global Leadership Summit. These men are working in areas often hostile to Christianity and have led through intense periods of persecution and civil war.

Africa and the Middle East

Africa

According to the *African Economist*, drawing on United Nations data, fifty cities in Africa have more than eight hundred thousand people. Lagos, Nigeria, is the largest with more than eight million. Kano, Ibadan, Kaduna, Port Harcourt, Benin, Maiduguri, and Zaria—all in Nigeria—are also among the fifty most populous cities in Africa.

Cairo, Egypt, is the second-largest African city, with approximately eight million people and a metropolitan population of more than fifteen million. Egypt also contains Alexandria, the fourth-largest African city. Kinshasa in the Democratic Republic of the Congo (DRC) is the third-largest, with more than six million people. The DRC has three other top-fifty cities, and South Africa has six. Nigeria, Egypt, the DRC, and South Africa together have twenty-two—nearly half—of the top fifty most populous cities on this huge continent, which comprises 20 percent of the earth's land mass—three times as large as the United States.[6]

Africa is a continent of great pain and great possibility. The population is expected to grow by 50 percent, the fastest-growing rate in the world, between 2010 and 2030.

According to Emmanuel Ndikumana, the Lausanne RD for Africa, living in Burundi, "The greatest challenges facing us are the fast growth of cities [and] serious infrastructure issues, including transportation and housing. Africa has a very young population, with the majority now under the age of fifteen. Unemployment causes a mass exodus to cities. When young people can't find work, the result is all sorts of economic and social problems: street children, sexual exploitation, and spread of HIV/AIDS."

The greatest sign of hope is that the church is growing rapidly. People have the freedom to preach the gospel in most of Africa. And many are coming to know the power and love of Christ, although all believers must be wary of those who preach a prosperity gospel. Those in northern Africa who follow Jesus often suffer intense persecution.[7]

The Middle East

The largest Middle Eastern cities include Istanbul, Tehran, Baghdad, Riyadh, Ankara, Jeddah, Kuwait City, Damascus, Dubai, Tel Aviv, and Jerusalem. No region in the world is as volatile spiritually and politically as the Middle East. The church here is diverse, with expressions of Coptic, Orthodox, Protestant, and Catholic believers. For the past three years, the advance of ISIS has presented enormous challenges to churches in the Middle East.

Andrea Zaki, the RD for the Middle East, describes the greatest challenges and hopes facing the area:

> Urbanization is a key influence in our region, and people migrate from rural communities to cities. People are seeking more freedom and economic prosperity. The outcome is that dreams are not fulfilled and many turn to religion as a shelter, creating radicalization.
>
> Spiritually we are living in a postmodern context. There is a strong movement among young people, as evidenced in the Arab Spring. For some, the result of the Arab Spring, when freedom and prosperity did not materialize, was disillusionment and a move toward atheism.
>
> Combining that with the impact of ISIS, there is great fear. Christians have shown great loyalty to their faith. Young people were slaughtered in Libya for their faith. ISIS will come to an end. It is terrorism based on disrespect to human dignity.
>
> What has given us hope is our historic confidence in the resurrection. At the cross there was no sign of hope, but in the resurrection there is always hope where there is no sign of hope. We have seen in recent years the removal of the Muslim brotherhood from power. We are also seeing economic progress.[8]

Europe and Eurasia

Europe

Europe is an enormous and complex continent, which can be thought of as three regions—northern, central/eastern, and southern Europe. Europe has more than forty nations and more than thirty major languages. According to Jean Paul Rempp, the

Europe RD, 196 million people live in the north, 130 million people live in the central and eastern areas, and 327 million people live in the south.

Major cities across the continent include London, Berlin, Gothenburg, Rome, Athens, Barcelona, Vienna, Krakow, Budapest, and Belgrade.

Regarding challenges to Europe, Rempp says,

> The landscape is changing dramatically with the influx of refugees from across the Middle East. Secularism has had a huge impact on Europe since World War II. In the northern countries, there is greater religious freedom. In the other parts of Europe, where evangelicals are minorities, there is much less freedom. This is especially true in the larger cities. Politicians rarely speak about religious things. Politicians are concerned about the spread of Islam. We see anti-Semitism and a dislike for evangelism. It is very difficult to get permission to lead public expressions of outreach.

However, signs of hope should not be ignored.

> The fastest-growing church in Europe right now is in France. Every ten days we see a new church being birthed. There are even signs of [spiritual] hunger among Islamic people in France. Many Muslims have been impacted by a Berber Christian leader we call the "Billy Graham of France." He has been instrumental in influencing Muslims toward Jesus.
>
> Europeans are tired after decades of materialism and secularism. We are seeing spectacular evangelism in Scandinavia [see chapter 17]. In Spain people are asking for more true religion. When they meet evangelicals they are more open. The All-European City Congress in Berlin in September 2015 is a great sign of hope for us. God is stirring across the continent.[9]

Eurasia

Eurasia is composed of the twelve former Soviet republics; the region includes Russia, Central Asia, and the Slavic nations. The premier city for Eurasia is Moscow; its leaders' decisions cause ripple effects throughout Eurasia. Several significant though lesser-known cities in Eurasia include Novosibinsk, Krasnodar, Kiev, and St. Petersburg.

According to Anatole Glukhovskyy, the RD for Eurasia, the greatest challenges for the region are building city and regional networks among churches and ministries. Low trust between diverse groups of churches and leaders is fairly apparent. Eurasian cities are confronted with secularism, and sharing the gospel in a secular context is challenging. This is a difficult time for younger leaders in Turkey, where the church is experiencing persecution.

Glukhovskyy lives in the Ukraine, which is facing the realities of having Russia as a neighbor. The political and military climate overshadows everything that happens in this region of the world.

But Glukhovskyy recognizes signs of hope, including a stronger, nationwide spiritual movement emerging in Ukraine. Business as mission is evolving as a powerful expression of the gospel. Businesspeople are being ordained to lead their companies and be a witness in the marketplace.[10]

The Americas

Latin America and the Caribbean

The largest cities in Latin America are Sao Paulo, Mexico City, Lima, Bogota, Rio de Janeiro, Santiago, Caracas, Buenos Aires, Salvador, Brasília, and Fortaleza. Five of the largest eleven cities in Latin America are in Brazil. Mexico City represents 25 percent

of Mexico's population.[11] Brazil's and Mexico's combined populations represent more than half of all Latin America.[12]

In the Caribbean, the thirty island countries with 33 million
people are divided into five language groups—French, Spanish,
English, Dutch, and Danish.

According to Las Newman, RD for the Caribbean, Jamaica
has become known as the "land of music and murder." On an
island of three million people, 86 percent of the children are
born out of wedlock—one of the highest rates in the world. The
chief burden facing the church in Jamaica and much of the Caribbean is taking responsibility for the social and spiritual needs
of local communities. Churches need to unite and live out the
Christian ethic. The church has existed for five hundred years
in the Caribbean and needs renewal.

"The poverty of the region is masked by its beauty," Newman
says. "Violence begets violence. In Jamaica alone there are 250
criminal gang networks. There is a transnational network, including Jamaica and Columbia, involved with [drug] trafficking."[13]

But, on the optimistic front, Christians are finding themselves strategically placed at heads of companies, and some in
the political arena. These leaders have the opportunity to bring
a fragmented church together. Pentecostalism is also growing
rapidly. One church in Kingston has eight thousand members.
Churches are addressing the needs for housing and economic development, and newer churches are reaching the urban lower class.

North America

I interviewed Tom Lin, the North American RD and director
of the Urbana Missions Conference. We discussed the challenge
of reaching millennial leaders (see chapter 7).

The majority of the US population—approximately 170 million people—lives in the forty largest metro areas. The majority of Canadians live close to the US border. Canada's five largest cities are Toronto, Montreal, Calgary, Ottawa, and Edmonton. In 2012, A.T. Kearney listed Toronto as the sixteenth most influential global city.[14]

Lin says the greatest challenge he sees in North America is the need for Christians to live in the public square rather than remain entrenched in their safe Christian "ghettos." InterVarsity and sister organizations like Cru and Navigators are challenging students to engage their faith and work as two integral aspects of the same life mission. Lin also acknowledges,

> I'm encouraged. Over the seventy-year history of Urbana, 280,000 students have participated. We see new graduates going to cities with both a mission commitment and a marketplace commitment to engage. Grads are living in intentional community with each other.
>
> Recent grads have a commitment to engage the poorest of the poor in their cities. We had two thousand students [involved] in urban projects this past year.
>
> We want to see much more happening in the area of evangelism on campuses among all of the groups. Our vision is to see one thousand chapters planted on campuses where there are none now. We want to link hands with all of the agencies doing this work to see what can be done.[15]

South Pacific

The most populous countries in the South Pacific are Australia, Papua New Guinea, and New Zealand. The eight largest cities in the region are Sydney, Melbourne, Brisbane, Perth, Adelaide, Auckland, Wellington, and Christchurch, collectively home to eighteen million people.

The South Pacific includes the regions of Melanesia, Polynesia, and Micronesia. Port Moresby in Papua New Guinea has five hundred thousand people, and Suva in the Fiji Islands is home to two hundred thousand. Noumea in New Caledonia is the largest French-speaking city, home to 180,000.

According to Charlie Fletcher, RD for the South Pacific, Australian cities face significant economic and social challenges. An aging population combined with the end of the mining boom bodes poorly for the country financially. Secularism and consumerism also present enormous issues. Many in the majority culture are struggling with the challenge of multiculturalism. Climate change and the response to asylum seekers pose moral concerns.

Fletcher sees several signs of hope, including the growth of evangelical churches against a backdrop of declining Christian numbers in the census. Multiple organizations together are pushing a church-planting effort. And the Hillsong worship movement has become a global phenomenon.

New Zealand has been a major source of missionaries within the region, and leaders in the country are attempting to bring together the broader Christian community to work together. Believers in New Zealand are wrestling seriously with issues of Christian and ethnic identity.[16]

WHAT THIS WORLD PICTURE TEACHES US:
Cities Disrupted by the Gospel

God is urbanizing the world.

That the global population will grow 20 percent in twenty years—with most of that growth in cities—demonstrates God's commitment to use cities as His vehicle to bring people to Him.

God is using the church in the majority world (Asia, Africa, and Latin America) to become a bigger and more powerful missionary force to the secular West. Despite the challenge of increased secularization in cities, community-oriented millennial leaders are moving into cities and becoming a growing presence.

The most challenged places are generating the most courageous leaders.

Christian leaders in countries like China, India, Ukraine, and Egypt are demonstrating tremendous courage in the context of persecution and suffering. God is raising up new voices in some extraordinarily dark places. Christian communities that have been anchored for thousands of years are persevering through current seasons of suffering.

God is full of surprises.

The unanticipated historic growth of the Chinese church, Muslims coming to Jesus throughout Europe, and the unique interconfessional partnerships emerging in new places are creating enormous hope.

Because most spiritual movements are started by leaders under twenty-eight—and the majority of the world is under twenty-five—there is reason to be optimistic that God is bringing about innovative developments we never could have anticipated.

A Prayer

Jesus,

> *As we attempt to look through Your eyes at the world and all of its possibilities and pain, open our hearts. Allow us to enter into Your grief for the war-torn cities of the Middle East,*

the despair of the refugees, and the numbness of the secularized marketplace leaders. Enlarge our hearts to understand the scope and breadth of the great cities of the world.

Show us each our unique assignments. Help us battle against the numbing effects of secularism in our own hearts and the temptation to live apart from those among whom You have placed us. Help us to show Your love to the specific neighborhood into which You have called each of us.

Amen.

AFTERWORD

THE GOSPEL IN THE MARKETPLACE

M y wife, Leslie, and I have become better acquainted and more deeply committed to gospel movements as a result of the 2010 Lausanne Congress on World Evangelism in Cape Town, South Africa. There I sat down with Tim Keller and Mac Pier to hear their vision for cities, and New York City in particular. The experience enlarged our vision and ignited our passion for reaching our world for Jesus Christ, especially through cities and the marketplace.

I challenge you, particularly you marketplace leaders, to fully engage in your cities, partnering with others as you more fully commit to this exciting movement. The gospel's growth in cities is directly proportionate to the visible leadership of marketplace leaders in those cities.

Billy Graham has said that the marketplace will be to the gospel in this century what the medical profession was to the gospel in the last century. If he's right, those of us in the marketplace have a high privilege and responsibility to be ministers—salt and light—where God has placed us. A calling to disrupt our cities.

God sometimes advances the gospel's disruption of cities by first disrupting our lives. I have been privileged with a challenging career in the investment management business for more than thirty-five years. At first I was a faithful but quiet witness. Recently I became more visible and vocal about my faith. But my life was radically disrupted in 2012, a year I'd prefer not to repeat but one I would not trade for anything. That May I lost my job, ostensibly for sharing my faith. The loss hit me hard, as I had unknowingly transferred some of my very identity to my work, so I suddenly felt lost.

Work/career/position had become an idol in my life. I came to recognize that it's a dead end to trust anything to deliver the control, security, significance, satisfaction, and beauty that only the one true God can give. For many of us, *doing* productively becomes an attempt at self-redemption. To paraphrase Tim Keller, "We all have treasures—the things we cherish, delight in, and adore above other things. To understand these idols is to understand the hierarchy of our souls and the foundation of our personalities." To quote the Master, "Where your treasure is, there your heart will be also" (Matt. 6:21). Because we set up idols in our hearts, we recognize that making an idolatrous image of something (see Exod. 20:4) is not necessarily a physical process but is certainly always a spiritual and psychological one. It means turning a good thing into an ultimate thing.

My time between jobs gave me a good but gut-wrenching opportunity to clarify God's calling in my life and to sense the rich fellowship in prayer and in presence with the body of Christ. I remember moping around the house one Saturday morning a few weeks after losing my job, wondering out loud, "What is God doing? What is God saying?" My wife suggested I view the hundreds of emails of support, prayer, and care I had received. That, she said, was what God was saying. We need one another, and I am newly and sincerely thankful for brothers and sisters in Christ who demonstrated deep caring during those days. God put me through this experience, in part, to increase my depth of compassion to do the same for others.

I formed a personal "board" of five guys who all love the Lord to pray for me, challenge me, hold me accountable, and help carry me to God's next station. I am grateful to God for those men—Mac Pier was one—His ambassadors at my time of uncertainty. I am now better equipped to serve in the workplace—fully cognizant of whose I am and who is on the throne—to speak in word, deed, and attitude for Him.

The gospel has to be lived out and communicated where people are if we hope to influence nonbelievers to consider Christ and His claims. This will happen in the communities in which Christians routinely find themselves. Most adult Americans spend most of their waking lives at their jobs, so the marketplace has long been the arena for Christians to live out their faith in ways that attract others to Christ.

What if all Christians working in schools, factories, construction sites, public and private offices, hospitals, shops, and banks saw themselves as God's kingdom ambassadors and were equipped by the church to live boldly as Jesus followers in the marketplace? In an increasingly multireligious, multicultural society that is skeptical about organized Christianity, don't you think seeing Christians live with integrity at work would endear more unbelievers to Jesus and His life-giving claims?

Cities feature connectivity—financial transactions, knowledge transference, media production—that provides the seedbed for social change. This isn't a new reality. Even Socrates once said, "The country places and the trees don't teach me anything, but the people in the city do." People are attracted to cities because cities are magnets for talent and ambition, even though people can work from nearly any location in our globalized, digital, virtual world.

Why has there not been more transformation of our cities? Keller has suggested it's because pastors and church leaders don't hold the business and government authority from which city change originates. Until we marketplace leaders act like ministers of the gospel in our respective posts, city transformation may stagnate. We're not just financiers of God's work—we can be significant catalysts for the transformation of lives. We've been called and prepared to share the gospel in word and deed with the lost and must not act like second-class citizens in God's redemptive plan.

The church is the people of God already deployed across all domains of culture. These marketplace assignments have been made by a God who desires to plant the incarnate presence of His Son everywhere, because God so loves *the world*, not just the church. We have the opportunity to be the church right where we already are. Marketplace leaders need to pray for our cities. Jeremiah 29:7 says, "Seek the peace and prosperity of the city. . . . Pray to the LORD for it, because if it prospers, you too will prosper."

In *Every Good Endeavor*, Keller argues that marketplace leaders (and all workers) are to seek excellence in the execution of our work responsibilities. We are to exhibit integrity, not sleaziness; to be savvy but not ruthless; to be generous, not stingy; and to be unflappable. Be excellent in your work, Tim exhorts, as we are ultimately working for God. This will give us credibility and respect—characteristics necessary for effectiveness in witnessing—among our co-workers. "Whatever you do, work at it with all your heart, as working for the Lord, not for human masters, since you know that you will receive an inheritance from the Lord as a reward. It is the Lord Christ you are serving" (Col. 3:23–24).

In *Chariots of Fire*, Eric Liddell explains to his sister why he intends to run in the Olympics: "When I run, I feel God's pleasure." God wants to use each of us in our sphere of influence for His pleasure. This means we need a godly work style, manifested in our attitudes, methods, language, and behavior. The apostle Paul reminded us, ambassadors for Jesus, that we emit the fragrance of Christ. The attitudes we wear to our workplaces should remind others of Jesus. The fruit of the Spirit—love, joy, peace, patience, kindness, goodness, faithfulness, gentleness, and self-control—should pervade our attitudinal fragrance.

- We need impeccable reputations for finances, caring, and commitment to others.
- We need to demonstrate consistent generosity with time and money, often by living below our potential lifestyles.
- We especially need to be calm and poised in difficulty or failure. That's when we're watched most carefully.
- We need to be identified as Christians in our workplaces, not just blend in.
- And at the same time we need to respect and treat as valued equals those who believe differently.

My decades in the marketplace and in senior leadership have convinced me that earning the right to be heard on anything—including our faith—starts with excellence in what we do. Who wants to listen to or emulate mediocrity?

Go deep with Him—the one who is sufficient and worthy of our loyalty, allegiance, and worship. He is worthy of our every Spirit-guided effort to make Him known. Amen.

Bob Doll, December 2015

NOTES

Chapter 1 A Disrupted Life: Seeds of a Movement

1. Wording borrowed from Willow Creek Community Church's Mission Statement, www .willowcreek.org/aboutwillow/what-willow-believes.

2. Timothy Keller, *Center Church* (Grand Rapids: Zondervan, 2012), 378–81.

Chapter 2 New York City Disrupted

1. Jonathan Edwards, *A Humble Attempt* (1747), Lord's Day, www.lords-day.org/resources _dl/edwards_humble.html.

2. Mac Pier, *The Power of a City at Prayer* (Downers Grove, IL: InterVarsity, 2002), 34.

3. Clifford Knowles, "New York Crime Rate Plummets to Levels Not Seen in 30 Years," *New York Times*, December 20, 1996.

4. Christopher Mathias, "New York City Murder Rate in 2013 Reaches Historic Low," *Huffington Post*, December 30, 2013, www.huffingtonpost.com/2013/12/30/new -york-city-murder-rate-2013_n_4520192.html.

5. Personal conversation with Jeffrey Burkes, as quoted in Pier, *Power of a City*, 34.

6. Pier, *Power of a City*, 38.

7. Carl Ellis, *Beyond Liberation* (Downers Grove, IL: InterVarsity, 1983).

8. Norris Magnuson, *Salvation in the Slums* (Grand Rapids: Baker, 1977).

Chapter 3 The Gospel Grows in Manhattan

1. Interview with Preston Washington, CEO, Harlem Congregations for Community Improvement, February 1998.

2. Timothy Keller, *Prodigal God* (New York: Dutton, 2008), xv.

3. Ibid., 36.

4. Interview with Robert Guerrero, church-planting catalyst, Redeemer City to City, New York, August 2015.

5. We learned this from an experienced church planter in one of our meetings.

6. Interview with Tony Carnes, president, Values Research Institute, March 2014.

7. Scott Kauffman, *The NYC Movement Project Prospectus, 2010*, 1, 3–4.

8. Mike Hales, Erik Peterson, Andrés Mendoza Peña, and Johan Gott, *2014 Global Cities Index and Emerging Cities Outlook: Global Cities, Present and Future*, 2, A.T. Kearney, www .atkearney.com/documents/10192/4461492/Global+Cities+Present+and+Future-GCI +2014.pdf/3628fd7d-70be-41bf-99d6-4c8eaf984cd5.

9. Stephen Um and Justin Buzzard, *Why Cities Matter* (Wheaton: Crossway, 2013), 29.

10. E. B. White, *Here Is New York* (New York: The Little Bookroom, 1949), 19–20.

11. Tony Carnes, "The Making of the Postsecular City. The Manhattan Evangelicals, Part 1," A Journey through NYC Religions, December 1, 2010, www.nycreligion.info /making-postsecular-city-manhattan-evangelicals-part-1.

12. Tim Keller, *New York City Movement Project* video (New York: Redeemer City to City, 2011).

Chapter 4 Movement Day: Toward Missional Unity

1. John R. W. Stott, The Lausanne Covenant, Lausanne Movement, 1974, www .lausanne.org/content/covenant/lausanne-covenant.

2. Mac Pier, *Consequential Leadership* (Downers Grove, IL: InterVarsity, 2012), 169.

Chapter 5 The Gospel in the Streets of NYC

1. Pier, *Consequential Leadership*, 169.

2. Kevin Palau, *Unlikely* (New York: Howard, 2015), xiii–xiv.

3. "History," CityServe Portland, last accessed March 10, 2016, www.cityservepdx .org/schools/community-connections-2.

4. Interview with Kevin Palau, Portland, OR, August 21, 2015.

5. Mayor Bill de Blasio, greeting at CityServe launch, Calvary Baptist Church, September 23, 2014.

6. Palau interview.

7. "About," New York CityServe, last accessed February 18, 2016, www.nycityserve .org/about.

8. Interview with Jim Bushovern, Hawthorne, NJ, August 17, 2015.

9. Palau interview.

10. Ibid.

11. Ibid.

Chapter 6 Movement Day Greater Dallas

1. Interview with Ray Nixon, equity portfolio manager, Barrow Hanley, Dallas, TX, March 23, 2015.

2. Greg Abbot, keynote speech, Russell H. Perry Free Enterprise Award Banquet, Anatole Hotel, Dallas, TX, December 2013.

3. Nixon interview.

4. Ibid.

5. James C. Denison, "Movement Day Going Global Fact Sheet," 1.

6. Nixon interview.

7. Ibid.

8. Ibid.

Chapter 7 Millennial Gospel Movement in Dallas

1. Interview with Grant Skeldon, president of Initiative, Dallas, TX, August 10, 2015.

2. Interview with David Ro, international deputy director for East Asia, Lausanne Movement, June 2015.

3. Daniel Burke, "Millennials Leaving Church in Droves," CNN, May 14, 2015, www.cnn.com/2015/05/12/living/pew-religion-study.

4. Comments by Elias Dantas, executive director for international relations, Nyack Seminary, in Global Kingdom Partner Network meeting, Bangalore, India, November 7, 2015.

5. Skeldon interview.

6. Marc Yoder, "Top 10 Reasons Our Kids Leave Church," Church Leaders, last accessed April 7, 2016, www.churchleaders.com/children/childrens-ministry-articles/166129-marc-solas-10-surprising-reasons-our-kids-leave-church.html.

7. Tim Keller, presentation to Manhattan church planters, New York City, March 2012.

8. Skeldon interview.

9. Ibid.

10. "Why Christians in Culture Matter," Initiative, July 29, 2015, www.initiative network.org/blog/the-significance-of-reconciliation-in-the-church-of-dallas.

11. Skeldon interview.

12. Ibid.

Chapter 8 Dallas, the Gospel, and Race

1. See Claude Alexander, "From Sympathy to Solidarity," address presented at 100 City Conference, Hilton Hotel, New York City, October 28, 2015.

2. Interview with Chris Simmons, Cornerstone Baptist Church, Dallas, TX, March 2012.

3. Interview with Froswa' Booker-Drew, national director of community engagement, World Vision, Dallas, February 2013.

4. Interview by Jim Denison of Wilson Goode, executive director, Amachi, at Movement Day New York City, October 2014.

5. Pier, *Consequential Leadership*, 129.

6. Monica Hernandez, "Dallas Pastors Trade Places to Help Bridge Racial Gap," *USA Today*, March 30, 2015, www.usatoday.com/story/news/nation/2015/03/30/dallas-pastors-swap-bridge-racial-gap/70673614.

7. Interview with Bryan Carter, senior pastor, Concord Baptist Church, Dallas, August 2015.

8. Ibid.

9. Samuel Smith, "Texas Pastors Swap Pulpits on Palm Sunday to Share the Gospel's Call for Christians to Lead Racial Reconciliation," *Christian Post*, April 1, 2015, www.christianpost.com/news/texas-pastors-swap-pulpits-on-palm-sunday-to-share-the-gospels-call-for-christians-to-lead-racial-reconciliation-136760.

10. Deborah Fleck, "Park Cities, Red Bird Pastors Switch Places to Aid Racial Understanding," *Dallas Morning News*, March 29, 2015, www.dallasnews.com/news/community

-news/park-cities/headlines/20150329-pastors-switch-places-to-emphasize-greater
-racial-understanding.ece.

11. Carter interview.

Chapter 9 Manila, the Gospel, and the Slums

1. Corrie DeBoer, *Global City Case Study*, report provided for use in 2016 Movement Day Global Cities, New York City, May 2015.

2. Jane Sutton, "Telling It on a Mountain," *World Vision Today*, Summer 1998.

3. Interview with Corrie DeBoer, Manila, Philippines, August 21, 2015.

4. Jason Mandryk, *Operation World* (Colorado Springs: Biblica, 2010), 683.

5. "For-Profit Education: The $1-a-Week School," *The Economist*, August 1, 2015, www.economist.com/news/leaders/21660113-private-schools-are-booming-poor-countries-governments-should-either-help-them-or-get-out.

6. DeBoer interview.

7. Ibid.

8. Ibid.

9. Mandryk, *Operation World*, 684.

10. Document provided by Bishop Noel A. Pantoja, national director, Philippine Council of Evangelical Churches, August 2015.

Chapter 10 Mumbai, the Gospel, and the Red-Light District

1. Interview with Arthur Thangiah, Mumbai, India, June 28, 2015.

2. Arthur Thangiah, "Kingdom Transformation to Upper-Class Urbanites in India" (doctoral dissertation, Bakke Graduate University, June 2010), 23.

3. "Global Sex Trafficking Fact Sheet," Equality Now, last accessed March 23, 2015, www.equalitynow.org/node/1010.

4. Interview with Vandana Kripalani, Mumbai, India, August 26, 2015.

5. Ibid.

6. Ibid.

7. Interview with Finny Philip, Udaipur, India, August 27, 2015.

8. Interview with Anand Mahadevan, Mumbai, India, August 24, 2016.

9. Thangiah, "Kingdom Transformation," 3.

10. Interview with Gul Kripalani, Mumbai, India, August 26, 2015.

11. Mahadevan interview.

12. Anand Mahadevan, "I, the Convert," *Outlook*, October 27, 2008.

13. Mahadevan interview.

14. See Pallavi Pengonda, "Just 928 Households Own 20 Percent of India's Wealth: BCG Report," *Mint*, June 17, 2015, www.livemint.com/Money/Fr3Jho4Yw0y6qAmjEfRNAP/BCG-wealth-report-928-Indian-households-own-a-5th-of-countr.html.

15. Mahadevan interview.

Chapter 11 Chennai, the Gospel, and an Apostolic Calling

1. Interview with Jeyakaran Emmanuel and Mark Visvasam, Chennai, India, August 25, 2015.

2. Nada Sewidan, "Poverty in Chennai," The Borgen Project, May 17, 2015, borgen project.org/poverty-chennai-india.

3. K. Praveen Kumar, "Chennai Big Hub of Human Trafficking," *Times of India,* November 11, 2008.

4. Pranitha Timothy, "Freedom, Justice, and Reconciliation," presentation at Converge conference, New Life Church, Chennai, India, June 29, 2015.

5. Somesh Jha, "Unemployment Up for Women in Major Cities," *Business Standard,* October 23, 2013, www.business-standard.com/article/current-affairs/unemployment -rate-for-women-up-in-major-cities-113102201003_1.html.

6. "Chennai Faces a Unique Pollution Challenge," Centre for Science and Environment, August 6, 2013, www.cseindia.org/content/chennai-faces-a-unique-pollution -challenge-%E2%80%93-pollution-levels-appear-be-low-or-moderate-are-.

7. Jeyakaren Emmanuel, "Blood, Sweat, and Tears of the Missionaries to Chennai," address presented at the Converge Conference, New Life Church, Chennai, India, June 29, 2015.

8. Chennai Transformation Network presentation at the Converge conference, New Life Church, Chennai, India, June 29, 2015.

9. Emmanuel and Visvasam interview.

Chapter 12 Dubai: The Manhattan of the Middle East

1. Joel Kotkin, "The World's Most Influential Cities," *Forbes,* August 14, 2014, www .forbes.com/pictures/edgl45ghmd/no-7-dubai.

2. Interview with Prem Nair, Dubai, United Arab Emirates, August 24, 2015.

3. Ibid.

4. Ibid.

5. Interview with Sona Kazanjian, Dubai, United Arab Emirates, July 2, 2015.

6. Learn more at Nehemiahproject.org.

7. This acronym stands for *Adhonep é a Associação de Homens de Negócio do Evangelho Pleno,* which is Portuguese for "Association of Full Gospel Businessmen." Visit www .adhonep.org.br.

8. Nair interview.

9. Interview with Santosh Shetty, Dubai, United Arab Emirates, July 2, 2015.

Chapter 13 Singapore: The Manhattan of Asia

1. Kotkin, "Most Influential."

2. Interview with Ezekiel Tan, general secretary, Bible Society of Singapore, Singapore, July 6, 2015.

3. Bobby E. K. Seng, *In His Good Time* (Singapore: Bible Society of Singapore, 2003), 330.

4. Ibid., 279–83.

5. Ibid., 304, 313.

6. Ibid., 285–86.

7. Tan interview.

8. "Curious about Us," Love Singapore, last accessed February 29, 2016, www.love singapore.org.sg/.

9. Seng, *In His Good Time,* 333–34.

10. Tan interview.

11. Ibid.

12. Ibid.

13. Edmund Chan, "How God Led Me to Start the Global Alliance," Global Alliance of Intentional Disciple Making Churches, last accessed February 29, 2016, www.idmc global.com/index.php/get-to-know-us/our-story.

14. Ibid.

15. Interview with Edmund Chan, founder, Global Alliance of Intentional Disciple Making Churches, Fairmont Hotel, Singapore, July 7, 2015.

Chapter 14 Port-au-Prince: Lazarus on Our Doorstep

1. Jacqueline Charles, "Tens of Thousands Still Living in Tents Five Years after Haiti Earthquake," *Miami Herald*, January 11, 2015, www.miamiherald.com/news/nation -world/world/americas/haiti/article6005817.html.

2. Interview with John Hasse, national director, World Vision Haiti, Port-au-Prince, Haiti, August 25, 2015.

3. Chiamaka Nwosu and Jeanne Batalova, "Haitian Immigrants in the United States," Migration Policy Institute, May 29, 2014, www.migrationpolicy.org/article/haitian -immigrants-united-states.

4. Don Golden, verbal reflections informally titled "The Case for Haiti" during meeting formulating the Decadal Strategy to Impact Haiti, New York City Leadership Center, Long Island City, NY, July 15, 2014.

5. Hasse interview.

6. Interview with Mullery Jean-Pierre, NY, July 14, 2015.

7. Ibid.

Chapter 15 Pretoria and Kigali: The Gospel in Urban Africa

1. Interview with Pastor Alan Platt, Gordon-Conwell Seminary, South Hamilton, MA, October 9, 2014.

2. Interview with Pastor Jurie Kriel, Pretoria, South Africa, December 21, 2015.

3. Purpose statement, "Missions: Global PEACE," Saddleback Church, accessed December 18, 2015, www.saddleback.com/connect/ministry/the-peace-plan/lake-forest.

4. Rick Warren, address to Rwandan leaders, Amahoro Stadium, Kigali, Rwanda, September 1, 2013, www.rwandaupdate.wordpress.com.

5. Interview with President Paul Kigame, presidential palace, Kigali, Rwanda, April 2013.

6. Willie Foote, "Reflections from Rwanda: Investing in One of the World's Fastest-Growing Economies," *Forbes*, February 23, 2015.

Chapter 16 The United Kingdom, the Gospel, and Gather

1. Kotkin, "Most Influential."

2. Interview with Roger Sutton, Manchester, United Kingdom, September 14, 2015.

3. Chimera (pseudonym), "How 100,000 Britons Have Chosen to Become Muslim," Stop Islamization of the World, last accessed March 2, 2016, www.siotw.org/news_english .item.143/how-100-000-britons-have-chosen-to-become-muslim.html.

4. Visit www.gather.global.

5. Sutton interview.

6. Ibid.

7. Ibid.

8. Ibid.

9. "What Is a Street Pastor?" Street Pastors, www.streetpastors.org/about-us/what-is-a-street-pastor.

10. Interview with Ram Gidoomal, London, March 17, 2015.

11. Sutton interview.

Chapter 17 Gothenburg and Berlin: The Gospel in Urban Europe

1. Mark Bixler and Michael Martinez, "War Has Forced Half of Syrians from Their Homes. Here's Where They've Gone," CNN, September 11, 2015, www.cnn.com/2015/09/11/world/syria-refugee-crisis-when-war-displaces-half-a-country.

2. Jim Denison, *God Is Not a Hobby*, Denison Forum on Truth and Culture (2012), 1, www.assets.denisonforum.org/pdf/books/god-is-not-a-hobby-the-fifth-great-awakening-and-the-future-of-america.pdf.

3. Interview with Tomas Brunegård, Gothenburg, Sweden, September 22, 2014.

4. Interview with Axel Nehlsen, executive director of Together for Berlin, July 30, 2015.

5. Christopher J. Wright, "Whole Gospel, Whole Church, Whole World," Lausanne Movement, last accessed March 23, 2016, www.lausanne.org/content/whole-gospel-whole-church-whole-world.

6. Nehlsen interview.

7. Ibid.

Chapter 18 A Global Snapshot of Cities

1. Mandryk, *Operation World*, 1, 22, 28, 46, 72.

2. See Mike Hales and Andrés Mendoza Peña, *2012 Global Cities Index and Emerging Cities Outlook*, A.T. Kearney, 3, www.atkearney.com/documents/10192/dfedfc4c-8a62-4162-90e5-2a3f14f0da3a.

3. Interview with David Ro, international deputy director for East Asia, Lausanne Movement, Gordon-Conwell Seminary, South Hamilton, MA, August 24, 2015.

4. Interview with Philip Chang, international deputy director for Southeast Asia, Lausanne Movement, Kuala Lumpur, Malaysia, August 24, 2015.

5. Philip interview.

6. "50 Largest Cities in Africa," *The African Economist*, December 20, 2012, www.theafricaneconomist.com/50-largest-cities-in-africa.

7. Interview with Emmanuel Ndikumana, international deputy director for Africa, Lausanne Movement, Bujumbura, Burundi, August 21, 2015.

8. Interview with Andrea Zaki, international deputy director for the Middle East, Lausanne Movement, Cairo, Egypt, August 24, 2015.

9. Interview with Jean Paul Rempp, international deputy director for Europe, Lausanne Movement, Lyon, France, September 14, 2015.

10. Interview with Anatole Glukhovskyy, international deputy director for Eurasia, Lausanne Movement, Kiev, Ukraine, August 24, 2015.

11. "List of Latin American Cities by Population," *Wikipedia,* last modified on November 20, 2015, www.en.wikipedia.org/wiki/List_of_Latin_American_cities_by _population.

12. Mandryk, *Operation World,* 46.

13. Interview with Las Newman, international deputy director for the Caribbean, Lausanne Movement, Kingston, Jamaica, August 19, 2015.

14. See Hales and Peña, *2012 Global Cities Index,* 3.

15. Interview with Tom Lin, international deputy director for North America, Lausanne Movement, Madison, WI, August 24, 2015.

16. Interview with Charlie Fletcher, international deputy director for the South Pacific, Lausanne Movement, Sydney, Australia, August 24, 2015.

Mac Pier is the founder and CEO of The New York City Leadership Center and was instrumental in founding the inaugural Movement Day conference. A resident of New York City since 1984, Mac lives in a diverse neighborhood with residents from more than one hundred ethnicities and attends church with people who speak sixty different languages. He is the author of *Spiritual Leadership in the Global City* and *Consequential Leadership*, coauthor of *The Power of a City at Prayer*, and a contributor to *Signs of Hope in the City*.